Louis Alexis Malik-Khanam

Six Years in Europe

Sequel to thirty Years in the Harem

Louis Alexis Malik-Khanam

Six Years in Europe
Sequel to thirty Years in the Harem

ISBN/EAN: 9783743337671

Manufactured in Europe, USA, Canada, Australia, Japa

Cover: Foto ©ninafisch / pixelio.de

Manufactured and distributed by brebook publishing software
(www.brebook.com)

Louis Alexis Malik-Khanam

Six Years in Europe

CONTENTS.

CHAPTER I.

                                                                                   PAGE

On board the *America*—The Marquis de Moustier and his suite—Diplomatic leave-taking—Fresh alarms—Free at last . . 1

CHAPTER II.

Athens—Effect of our arrival—The Greeks and the Turks—The Candian insurrection—Danger ahead—Resolution to leave Athens 12

CHAPTER III.

An unpleasant discovery—Low condition of our finances—Friends in need and deed—Arrival in Paris 27

CHAPTER IV.

Appeal to M. de Moustier—His envoy—I apply to the Turkish Chargé d'Affaires—Hussein Bey—Arrival in Paris of Mehemet-Djemil Pasha 35

CHAPTER V.

Visitors from the Pope—The Abbé Boré—My landlord and the Turkish Embassy—I escape a snare 49

CHAPTER VI.

Ayesha's instruction in religious matters—Her notions of the Christian faith—Her baptism—The Ottoman Embassy still at

CHAPTER VII.

I renew my appeals to my husband—The Sultan's visit to Paris—I find myself in a new dilemma—We go to Fontenay-aux-Roses—My husband's duplicity—We are taken into the convent of the Sisters of Charity—Our experiences there—We leave the convent 81

CHAPTER VIII.

Fresh disappointments—Saġd Acha, the bankrupt merchant—A new acquaintance—Ayesha receives an offer of marriage—We take a journey into Brittany—Our host—Mysterious incidents—Ayesha accepts the proposal for her hand 105

CHAPTER IX.

We go to London—My daughter's marriage—We return into Brittany—I am watched—I evade M. Questel's vigilance—My new relations—Extraordinary revelations 129

CHAPTER X.

I impart to Ayesha her husband's history—We are invited to a family festival—A domestic crisis—More revelations—I have an explanation with my son-in-law 149

CHAPTER XI.

M. Questel's ill-treatment of me—Ayesha in terror—Violent scenes at home—M. Questel throws off the mask—The plot against myself and Ayesha revealed . . . 165

CHAPTER XII.

Further mystery at the Château de Kerbeque—Fresh revelations concerning my son-in-law—His projects and counter-projects—We return to Paris 176

CHAPTER XIII.

A disclosure relating to Ayesha's marriage—Monsieur Questel refuses to have it legalised—A visit to the Procureur Impérial with the Princess Davidoff—The result 183

CHAPTER XIV.

Monsieur Questel's vacillation—I am sent to Vienna—I return to Paris and am sent to Rome—Interview with Fuad Pasha—Departure for Paris 192

CHAPTER XV.

My journey to Geneva—Misadventures by the way—Monseigneur de Marseilles and Sister Josephine of the Convent of La Grande Miséricorde 204

CHAPTER XVI.

My first night in Lyons—My wanderings in search of a shelter—The hospital for the destitute—My fellow-patients—Night scene in my ward—Succour from Paris 215

CHAPTER XVII.

My return to Paris—My daughter's arrival—Monsieur Questel's excuses—A new personage appears on the scene—We leave for Messina with Monsieur Questel—His change of plan—He tries to lure us to Constantinople, and, as we will not go, he proceeds thither himself—The issue, and the last of M. Questel . 229

CHAPTER XVIII.

Changed demeanour of the Greeks towards us—Deceitful conduct of the French Vice-Consul—Attempt to inveigle us on board a Turkish war steamer—We are in danger from foot-pads—We receive an offer of a tour into the interior—Facts and inferences—We leave for Corfu 249

CHAPTER XIX.

From Corfu to Trieste—Haida Effendi's strange request—He is baffled—We reach Trieste—Visits to Haida Effendi—His proposals—How we got to Paris 263

CHAPTER XX.

Conversations with Haida Effendi upon matters personal to myself 274

CHAPTER XXI.

How I came to write a book—How I set about it, and how I fared—The war—We leave Paris for Brussels—Misadventure by the way—An old acquaintance suddenly crops up . . 292

CHAPTER XXII.

My landlady and "La Lanterne"—An old acquaintance suddenly crops up—We go to London—We get into mysterious company—Our visit to the Turkish Ambassador . . 307

CHAPTER XXIII.

Monsieur Alphonse and his friends—Singular and suspicious incidents—One of my husband's body-guard turns up in an unexpected manner—Last visit to the Turkish Ambassador—I determine to go away—Scene with my daughter—We part 317

CHAPTER XXIV.

The last blow 326

CHAPTER I.

On board the America—The Marquis de Moustier and his suite—Diplomatic leave-taking—Fresh alarms—Free at last.

"FREE!"—This was our first thought and exclamation on finding ourselves safely on board the *America*, the name of the mail steamer about to convey us to the Western world. "Free!"—Yet not wholly out of danger. We had fortunately evaded the police; we had obtained our passage-tickets without difficulty; but various unexpected accidents and contingencies might even now defeat our hopes. To conceal ourselves, then, until we should be well out of immediate peril, was our first impulse.

We hurried below, and huddled ourselves up in a corner of the ladies' cabin, where we crouched, rather than sat, tormented with anxiety, forestalling every possible mishap; nevertheless breathing more freely, inspired with the hope of ultimately effecting our escape.

None save those who have been similarly circumstanced, who have panted between the prospect of freedom or of a life-long imprisonment, can possibly realize our emotions. Every sound, the echo of every fresh voice, the trampling of new-comers upon the deck, all these gave rise to ever-changing feelings, which culminated, almost in horror, when we heard pronounced the name of the Marquis de Moustier. With him came Madame la Marquise, their two daughters, their son, a secretary, a governess, and a suite. I knew him as French Ambassador to the Sublime Porte, but he did not know me. I was also aware he had been appointed Minister of Foreign Affairs, and that his departure for Paris would not long be delayed; but I could not anticipate that he and his family would be our fellow-passengers, our companions in our flight. Should we be discovered, and a demand for our surrender be made, it was to be apprehended he would elect to hand us over to those who claimed authority over us as our legal guardians, rather than involve himself, at that particular moment, in any diplomatic dilemma, by asserting the inviolability of his flag. This mischance was most embarrassing, and, not feeling secure from intrusion, we drew all the closer together in our little corner, Ayesha trembling with terror.

But another and, in our position, a more terrible surprise awaited us, although M. de Moustier's presence on board ought to have, in a measure, prepared us for it. As Imperial Ambassador to the Porte, returning to Paris to assume the direction of foreign affairs, the Marquis was too mighty a personage to be allowed to quit Constantinople without special marks of attention. Scarcely had he and his suite set foot on board, than Ali Pasha, our Minister for Foreign Affairs, accompanied by my husband—then a member of the Council of Ministers—followed by his brother-in-law, our good friend Bessim, presented themselves for a final leave-taking.

Assuredly if my lord and, according to Oriental custom, my veritable master, had known that only a very few inches of plank then separated him from the wife and the children he was hunting down with such steady energy and vigilance, we should soon have been placed under the safest escort for the nearest prison—his own palace—antecedent to incarceration for life in an underground dungeon.

By another strange coincidence, his son, Djehad, repudiated and rejected, an outcast, and, like ourselves, a fugitive, beheld him on this occasion for the last time. Djehad had half concealed himself behind a mast, and thus had the opportunity of witnessing the ceremonious adieus of the group collected, in a circle, around M. de Moustier, and of gazing once more—and, as it proved, for ever in this world—upon the author of his existence. Djehad durst not move from his hiding-place, though he afterwards confessed he felt impelled, at one moment, to cast himself at Kibrizli's feet, and plead for us all for deliverance from further persecution.

The sound of these hostile voices set the heart of myself and of my daughter beating violently. My poor Ayesha clung to me as though I could shield her from the greatest evil that could befall her—once more falling into the arms of her father—and I embraced her all the more closely, because I felt my own utter helplessness to protect her from the violence of her natural guardian, should he discover us, and assert his despotic authority.

We thought the parting civilities of the great men would never terminate; but even the world must come to an end; and we were finally enabled to offer to the Mysterious Being, to whom all hearts instinctively turn in the hour of danger or of deliverance from peril, our fervent thanks that the exigencies of the mail service were paramount to those of diplomatic courtesy.

The signal-bell for departure, the revolving of the paddle-wheels, the sensation of motion after what seemed an eternity of agony, revived our spirits and our courage. Cramped in our cabin, longing for air—for that sun-light we felt was for us, was even exclusively our own—we at length ventured first to peep out, like mice looking if the coast is clear of cats. The noise of feet caused us to shrink back. It was only Djehad, who came to tell us we were passing Seraglio Point. Thus encouraged we came out, and went on deck.

How thrilling was the sensation of freedom! To be free to move whither we liked—unveiled to breathe the air—unveiled to gaze at the sun, at the sky, at all the bright beauties of nature—at objects fast receding from view, but with which our eyes were so familiar!

As we descended the "Great Straits," every minute drawing more and more beyond danger, further and further from the immediate reach of that terrible, silent, fiery messenger, the telegraph, our spirits rose and our courage grew. To Ayesha, everything was novel, and much was startling. It was odd to her to appear before everybody with her face uncovered, and she shrank from the inquisitive gaze of the menfolk on board; for, to exhibit her face thus openly was so contrary to her habits, to her education, and to her belief, that to do so was not quite harmless.

It is well known that Oriental custom, prejudice, creed, superstition—by whatever name it may be called—despotically insists that a woman shall keep her face veiled before men. The custom is oppressive, particularly when the weather is warm; and more particularly still when accident creates the opportunity of indulgence in that common, superlatively amiable, feminine foible, coquetry. A young girl, walking demurely by the side and under the guard of an elderly companion, is surely not so very much to blame, if, finding the heat oppressive, she throws up the veil which conceals her face, and more than a fair proportion of her shoulders, just at the very exact moment a young fellow is approaching —by the merest accident, of course—upon whom the sudden disclosure of her beauty may produce a lasting effect. Such a device is common in the East, as a means of evading the Prophet's injunction.

May I be permitted to add, that as against human nature—feminine human nature at any rate—I consider Mahomet made a grand mistake in this matter of prohibiting a woman to be unveiled in presence of the opposite sex. I am sorry to avow it, but I cannot help, as a woman, ranging myself on the side of human nature against Mahomet. He himself has said: "There is only one God, and Mahomet is His Prophet." Now, God conceived human nature before he created man; wherefore human nature dates before Mahomet. I must, therefore, believe first in human nature. If the teaching of Mahomet is contrary thereto, so much the worse for the Prophet.

We esteemed it a most fortunate circumstance there were on board comparatively few passengers. We were, none the less, objects of attention. Women are inquisitive by instinct. In the harem we have little else to do but to study female character. It has many bright sides when the passions are not in question; but, under all circumstances, inquisitiveness is the predominant trait. Thus the men took no particular notice of us. Accustomed to see many travellers, they probably perceived in us, dressed as we were in European costume, nothing especially remarkable. The Marquis de Moustier may have been observant, notwithstanding he was a diplomatist: by which I mean, that, according to my experience, diplomatists are, as a rule, less observant than they ought to be, or than they obtain credit for. One of them at our Court, whose nationality I abstain from recording, noticed nothing, yet gained a reputation for observing everything. But then he was very fortunate in his servants.

In our Oriental proverbiology we have the saying "As is the master so is the domestic." I have found this to be the reverse of the fact, for masters cannot play the part of spies; they have not the opportunity of investigating the petty intrigues which afflict their households, and which so frequently—as I shall have occasion to illustrate—bring about catastrophes involving them, and sometimes the fate of a nation. On the other hand, subordinates are all eyes and ears. They fetch, carry, tattle, and calumniate. We escaped M. de Moustier's diplomatic eye, so far as he gave any sign to the contrary, but were soon fastened upon by the governess.

I might, myself, have easily passed muster in a crowd, or out of one. Ayesha, however, could not fail to challenge attention. The character of her beauty was strikingly Oriental. Her large Eastern eyes flashed with light from beneath her grand arched eyebrows, and her long black eyelashes. No art could disguise the rich masses of her raven-coloured hair, or alter the symmetrical oval of her countenance. Her very carriage was peculiar; for, let me say **here, no woman** brought up in the harem knows how to walk. The gait is something between a waddle and a shuffle. Then, the utter freedom of her manners from the conventional restraints of what is called civilized society, was of itself sufficient to attract more than passing notice. No wonder then, our group soon became the centre towards which the governess gravitated.

The lady hovered around us a little, then made her first overtures by timidly taking a seat near us. As I spoke French sufficiently well for ordinary conversation, the prospect of a fine passage to Piræus was the colloquial aperient she administered to me.

Ah, indeed! To Athens! **then—then**? How far westward did we intend to travel? Had we come from the interior? **Did we** know many people in Constantinople? The gentleman yonder, **and the** lady **by** his side, were **the** Marquis and the **Marquise** de Moustier! Would we like to be introduced? In such case, she would be enchanted to undertake that office.

I fully understood **that these** and **a variety of** other questions were put with the astute view of drawing me **out.** The replies **she** obtained **at** first, were as brief as politeness demanded, and amounted to this :—

"We were Turkish ladies, on their travels. We should decide at Athens how much further west we might go. We were charmed to hear we had such distinguished fellow-passengers. We were not known to M. or to Mme. de Moustier, and an introduction to them did not appear necessary."

More I did not then care to impart. I still had before me the fear of re-capture, which I felt might result from the slightest imprudence on my part. But the lady was persevering as well as inquisitive. The fancy she took to my daughter was amazing in its demonstrativeness, and as we gradually left danger in the rear, and travelling unavoidably draws people into a degree of familiarity difficult to avoid without appearing boorish, my reserve wore off by little and little, and I at last told her we were effecting our escape from Turkey, and that our ultimate destination was Paris; but I did not disclose our name. Her interest in us, and her surprise, then exceeded all bounds, and when she quitted us, it was, as I understood, to communicate the intelligence to her superiors.

It may have interested them, for aught I know to the contrary; but they certainly took no observable interest in us, nor did they even speak to us. If I must confess the truth, I felt pleased at this, and rather relieved than otherwise, for I might have been betrayed into a conversation more or less prematurely confidential, which it was desirable, for many reasons, to avoid. Not until we reached Piræus did I feel we were really out of danger.

We arrived at Piræus about mid-day, our next stage being Athens. I was rejoiced to learn that our stay at Piræus would not exceed an hour. It is a much frequented summer bathing-place, but its general aspect disappointed me. The dwellings and the public buildings presented no striking characteristics, and the inhabitants appeared to me to be of a low type, were offensively unclean in person, and uncouth in manner.

The hour proved a long one, and pleased enough were we when the carriage which was to convey us to Athens at last drew up at the door of the hotel, and we were summoned to take our places in it.

CHAPTER II.

Athens—Effect of our arrival—The Greeks and the Turks—The Candian insurrection—Danger ahead—Resolution to leave Athens.

From Piræus to Athens is a two hours' ride, along a narrow, wretchedly kept-up road; if a road can be called kept-up which is in a chronic condition of unrepair. The dust was fine as well as abundant, so that we seemed to be moving through a mist, and very soon became coated with a greyish-white covering as though our latest employment had been grinding flour of indifferent quality. Nevertheless our gaiety was boisterous, for we were as free as that very dust we were compelled to inhale, and for freedom's sake rather enjoyed than otherwise. The scenery was not attractive; but the sensation of perfect freedom lent it an extrinsic charm, which more than compensated for natural deficiencies. Olive-tree plantations and vineyards alternated all along the road, which now ascending, brought us upon what seemed interminable plains, then dipping, plunged us into green valleys, fresh and cool, but also apparently never ending. The fact is, we were impatient to reach Athens, which at last appeared in sight. We got down at the Hôtel de la Grande Bretagne, situated immediately opposite the King's palace, and, according to custom, we inscribed our name in the register kept for visitors. Little did I imagine the sensation that very simple formality would create. Kibrizli-Mehemet Pacha was a Prince of Cyprus, and born there, consequently his name was well-known, apart from the fact of his high official position. I had never thought of this. Even if I had, I should probably not have concealed my name and quality. No sooner did these transpire, than the landlord informed us, with every outward manifestation of consideration and courtesy, that our flight having been discovered, telegrams from Constantinople had come intimating the fact to the Turkish Ambassador. I received the intimation with the greatest indifference, knowing I was quite safe now, and that my presence would be rather agreeable than otherwise to the Greek party. At the table-d'hôte—which I may state was in the Oriental style, most profuse and magnificent, and frequented, not only by the guests staying in the hotel, but by the grandees and notabilities of the metropolis—we were the centre towards which all eyes turned. The balcony of our apartments overlooked the great square, crowded by the population, who flock hither to drink coffee, and to listen to the music, which every evening, as well as every morning, plays in front of the King's residence. When we came out upon the balcony, a new excitement seemed to pervade the crowd. The news of our arrival had soon spread, and our flight—probably exaggerated in its details—our rank, our peculiar position, already constituted us objects of special interest to this easily moved people. Next morning the newspapers contained articles concerning us, and we at once became the celebrities of the hour. Visits from all the distinguished personages in the city poured in upon us. It became quite a rivalry who should be most courteous. The King's first equerry, amongst others, found his way to us, and inquired if we needed anything, what were our plans and intentions, and when, and how, and why we had fled from Constantinople. The Secretary of the Turkish Ambassador also came. The latter—Fotiare Bey—was a Greek, in the employ of the Turkish Government, and brother-in-law of Musurus, Ambassador to the Court of St. James', each having married daughters of Prince Vogorivi, of Samos. He was sent specially to ascertain why we had come to Athens, and he was also the bearer of an invitation for us to pay the Ambassador a visit. As I knew that Greeks in the Turkish service are not to be trusted, I felt seriously suspicious of overtures from this quarter, and made up my mind resolutely to decline them. This I did at once, very courteously, and with a profusion of thanks, and explaining that we had quitted home in anger. He remonstrated, and observed, that such being the case was a reason for our returning: a hint I immediately perceived had not come unsuggested, and which confirmed my suspicions and my conviction. My reply was that we did not intend going back to Constantinople, but to proceed on our travels westward, as far away from it as possible. We should remain a short time in Athens, and then resume our journey.

Amongst other habitual frequenters of our grand table-d'hôte was an old man of eighty-four, handsome, and of a most noble and imposing aspect, who adhered to the old Greek costume, and to the traditional courteous and polished manners of his ancestry. He had formerly been Minister of Marine, and was father-in-law of the then Minister of Foreign Affairs. Incidentally I gleaned from him—as well as from others—that the Greek Government would help me if I felt disposed to claim its aid; and this, only to be disagreeable to the authorities at the Porte. But I did not see my way to adopt such a medium of endeavouring to procure means of living, which was now, after nearly a month's stay in Athens, becoming the chief object of my thoughts, night and day.

My daughter seemed so completely happy in her novel position, that I felt averse to mar her felicity by any reference to coming necessities and troubles; at least, until it should be absolutely unavoidable to recall her to a sense of the realities of the hour. As for plans, I had formed none very determinate; but as the days wore on, and I recovered from the fatigue and the anxiety I had undergone, my spirits rose, my courage revived, and my mind recovered its elasticity and activity. Thus, from day to day, pondering over my position, I gradually came to the final determination to proceed to Paris, and claim the friendly interposition of the French Government to induce my husband either to allow us a fixed annual income, or to give up the jewels, securities, money, and title-deeds of properties settled upon myself and my daughter in our own right. I considered I had a perfect right to claim French interference in my behalf in virtue of my father's French descent.

Then, I believed in justice!

Our time in Athens, meanwhile, was passing away pleasantly enough. We went out daily to inspect the monuments, and to see the sights. These latter were simply the incidents in the everyday life of the people. We made purchases, we frequented the public promenades; we contracted acquaintances, if we did not make friends. We also gained experience in numerous ways. We soon discovered that the shop and stall-keepers possessed a conscience of astounding elasticity in all matters of trade, and would demand three and four times the worth of any article offered for sale; a price we, in our lamentable ignorance, at first paid. The value of money to us was absolutely unknown, and we did not suspect that knavery was a common element in business amongst these fair-spoken, smooth-tongued Greeks.

We were not long in ascertaining that hospitality does not figure amongst the national characteristics. In Turkey, to entertain is the rule. We found our Greek lady-acquaintances ready enough, even eager, to accept all kinds of courtesies at our hands, when they visited us; but they never favoured us in a similar way. The fact is, pride lay at the root of their apparent churlish selfishness. In their case, the stomach suffers for the back. Their homes are not for strangers to see. Everything is sacrificed to outward show. A lady wearing gorgeous attire, and resplendent with jewels, shrinks from exposing the misery of the domestic interior, often squalid to the last degree. This absence of hospitality struck us painfully, for in Turkey even the poorest share with the stranger. Indeed, I was now prepared to find that in Europe I must not expect to meet with hospitality upon the grand scale common in my own country. I confess that even when I discovered the cause of its absence in Athens—at least amongst the class I have designated—I felt disappointed, even a little mortified, interpreting it as a personal slight. I was simply over-sensitive in my forlorn and peculiar position. At any rate, the prospect of being shut out from any kind of domestic intimacy with Greek female society had its influence in deciding me to make no prolonged stay where we were.

The Greek Patriarch, with whom we were on visiting terms, expressed a strong desire, some anxiety even, that we should remain. He had taken part in the war in the Morea; was full of anecdote, highly agreeable, and chatted well. We made his acquaintance through one M. Delaporte, formerly Greek Consul at Aivalik. Like many others, he believed in the ultimate success of the Candian insurrection, then at its height, and considered Russian intervention as certain. I held totally opposite views, knowing the power of the Turks. The Patriarch was most kind, and again and again offered us help, but I declined with many and most sincere thanks.

We very frequently saw the young King on the public promenade. His countenance is intelligent, and his bearing distinguished. He always wore a smile on his lips, and saluted the multitude with the greatest affability. He struck me as being far from proud. I often thought of this young King ruling in so old a country, and wondered whether they would grow and thrive together. He has no easy task before him, for the Greeks are a most difficult people to govern. Honesty, patriotism, public virtue, national spirit, are things unknown. Selfishness reigns paramount. In fact, the Greek element is essentially false.

Between the Greeks and the Turks, not the smallest particle of love is lost. The Turks are glad to secure the services of the Greeks, because these people are so pliant, accommodating, and obsequious. In Constantinople, where the Greeks swarm, and their influence makes itself felt, there is much less frankness and fair dealing than in the provinces. Self-interest is the link which brings both into association; but at bottom Greek hates Turk, and Turk hates Greek. That this is the predominant popular sentiment admits of no doubt whatsoever.

The character of the people impresses itself upon the national policy, as a matter of course. Hence, that of the Greek Government is sly, underhand, dark, dubious, and false. The plan of the Cretan insurrection, to wit, was known at Athens, notoriously known, long before it broke out, but the authorities, the diplomatists, knew nothing about it, or rather, affected the most splendid ignorance. I do not know to what origin the Candian insurrection was ascribed generally in Europe. In political circles in Athens it was traced to an intrigue between the French Emperor and Kalergi, a Greek, a orfmer equerry of King Otho's, and who was on the friendliest terms with Louis Napoleon. Kalergi is said to have solicited some mark of personal favour at the hands of the Emperor, who offered to make him Prince of Candia if Crete could free herself from Turkish dominion. This promise set Kalergi to work, and the insurrection commenced. Kalergi, however, discovered that the Emperor sought Crete for France, whereas Kalergi's purpose was to secure it for Greece, and finding that French aid, secretly agreed to be given, did not come, he abandoned the contest.

I give this report as it reached me, without offering any opinion upon its accuracy. I can only record that whatever may have been the origin of the movement, much deep though quiet enthusiasm existed in its favour. If the Candians won, Greece would benefit by the gain of an additional province; but openly to interfere on the side of the insurrectionists, would have been to incur the full-blown hostility of the Turks; in a word, to provoke, on a grand scale against the whole of Greece, a war which was actually then confined only to a rebellious corner of the Ottoman Empire.

The Greek authorities, nevertheless, secretly encouraged the insurrectionists, whilst openly condemning the insurrection. Hundreds of men, whose destination was notorious, unarmed and unequipped, were continually leaving Athens at night; and a stream of wounded was as constantly flowing back, including numerous women, who had fought by the side of their husbands, their sons, or their fathers.

Some of them had children. When these wounded warriors arrived, the landing-place and its neighbourhood would be thronged by crowds, to welcome them back, to ask news of the absent, and to encourage the suffering. These were at once conveyed away into private houses as well as to the hospital, to be tended and cared for. The spectacle was a really touching one, and moved me greatly. I felt persuaded the sacrifices made would prove useless, the Turks being in every respect superior in strength to the Greeks as a nation, and therefore necessarily so to the Candians. I gave this, as my opinion, to the Greek Patriarch, who, as I have stated, held opposite views, and looked and hoped for Russian intervention.

I may say, whilst upon this subject, that I have more faith in the future of Greece than of Turkey. I regard Turkey not as a sick man, that is, a man likely to recover health and strength, but as one absolutely dying of consumption, and whose last agony is a mere question of time. Turkey in Europe is an anomaly, and Constantinople is the natural geographical capital of Russia, which she will assuredly obtain some day, perhaps not so far distant. Turkey will then be thrown wholly back into Asia, upon which territory her institutions may find room and opportunity to develope amongst peoples of kindred religion; though it seems to me utterly impossible she can ultimately resist the inroads of Christian civilization. On the other hand, Russia must grow European Turkey out of Europe. She knows how to wait, and though, when her time comes to assume possession of Constantinople, she will probably enlarge the boundaries of Greece, she was not likely, at the time of the Candian insurrection, to take the false step of interfering in that contention, notwithstanding that her sympathies may have secretly tended that way.

Holding these convictions, and foreseeing the result of the war, I concluded that, with peace, the authorities in Athens would seek to be as complaisant as possible to the ruling powers at Constantinople, and that my husband and his relatives would find in Athens instruments to their hand, willing to promote their object of getting us back to the Turkish capital. I may have been over-timorous, but my recent sufferings fully justified any exaggeration of present fears, and I at length disclosed to my daughter my intention of quitting Athens.

This announcement suddenly aroused her to the realities of our position. We had been a month in that city; she as utterly oblivious of the past as though it were a forgotten dream. Young, entirely guileless of the world, released from the caged-up, monotonous life of the Harem, with all its terrible restraints upon the mind as well as the body, she found herself all at once in a new sphere, which to her was Paradise. The commonest incidents of the life we were leading, were to her so many new enjoyments, and new sensations. It was a delight to be able to go about whither, and how, and when she listed; to speak and to be spoken to without fear. The very attempt to make herself understood—she had picked up a little French—had its charm, and its amusement. Especially did she revel in the luxury of an unveiled face; of breathing the air without impediment, and in the novel indulgence of looking at those who looked at her.

So wholly was she carried away by pleasurable emotions, so absorbed was she in the luxurious felicities of her new life, that it cost me the severest pang to interrupt the current of her happiness. Had I listened to her entreaties, we should have remained in Athens. Were we not very happy? Had we not everything we needed? Were we not free? Were we not safe? Could we not communicate with her father as easily from where we were as from any other city? These and similar questions were pressed upon me, mingled with caresses and entreaties. It proved a task to convince her of the necessity of our breaking away from present temporary enjoyments, in order to secure permanent prospective advantages. Then, was not Paris our destination and the haven of our hopes? There we should find the attractions and pleasures of Athens, multiplied a hundred-fold. In that centre of civilization, that resort of all the notabilities of the world—about to become a universal fair at which the industries of all the nations would be displayed—she would enjoy the fullest opportunity of indulgence in her tastes, of augmenting her occupations, of enlarging her experience, of contracting friendships, of acquiring the education she so sorely needed to enable her to hold her own amongst her equals; she would see the best of society in its most decorous attire, and on its foremost best behaviour; she would mix with it herself, on an equality with the highest, having me constantly by, to guide and watch over her, to protect as well as love her. "And, my child," I added, "you shall then carry out your desire to embrace the Christian faith; and who knows you may not find a new and a good husband?"

These arguments prevailed. Whether the last had special weight I cannot positively assert, nor will I hazard a suspicion it had none. I was too pleased to perceive they had overcome a reluctance I at one moment apprehended might prove indomitable; for I must here avow the fact: I had experience of my self-willed girl: a mere child in everything save her twenty-one years and her troubles.

CHAPTER III.

An unpleasant discovery—Low condition of our finances—Friends in need and deed—Arrival in Paris.

I HAVE observed we had no idea of the value of money. My stock of this indispensable commodity was not by any means considerable, even on our arrival, and was now greatly diminished by purchases of indispensable articles for our modern toilet, and of nick-nacks, of dubious utility no doubt, but which added to my daughter's pleasure by gratifying her wishes. When I requested our hotel-bill to be sent up, I had no notion whether the balance of cash in hand would suffice to meet the demand, or would exceed it; nor had I reflected what I should do in the event of a deficiency. The memorandum was presented in due course. It amounted to seventeen hundred francs; sixty-eight pounds sterling: balance in the exchequer, fifty francs: two pounds! I paid the bill, and we quitted Athens once more for Piræus.

To take the first steamer for Marseilles was an absolute necessity. It was to start within forty-eight hours, and I determined to proceed by it. Our arrival soon became known. In the hotel we had selected dwelt the American Consul, who requested permission to pay us a visit. He was followed by the Russian, the French, and three other functionaries of the same class. The French Consul, hearing of my intention to go to Marseilles without delay, gave me an introductory letter to his colleague there, and one to the Emperor's chamberlain in Paris. These were very acceptable.

The Consuls followed up their civilities by inviting us to a banquet, got up jointly by them in our honour, and to which we gladly went. Had we been travelling in state, in the full tide of our splendour, instead of being only two poor fugitives, homeless and penniless, the ovation could not have been more magnificent. We were leaving the next morning, and as I wished to do so unceremoniously, I did not inform these gentlemen at what hour I should proceed on board. My luggage was not bulky, only one large trunk, and we preceded it to the steamer quite early. But our courteous friends the Consuls were not disposed to permit us to slip away so quietly; and followed us a little later, arriving, however, in ample time to give their leave-taking quite the character of a ceremonial. It probably had its effect later, when to be known as somebody, was not without its advantage, as the sequel will show.

I never entertained a doubt that upon presenting to the French Consul at Marseilles the letter of introduction of which I was the bearer from his colleague at Athens, I should be able to obtain wherewith to pay our sea-passage to the former place, and our railway-fare thence to Paris. Nevertheless, the alternative was unpleasant; but there was no help for it in our position. To reach Paris was imperatively necessary, and I trusted that my papers, establishing my identity as well as my rank and quality, would inspire the Captain with sufficient confidence to trust me for our passage-money, until I should have tested the value of my credentials upon the French Consul.

I found, upon investigating the contents of my purse, that the discharge of my hotel bill had left me with only two francs.

I presume that the great civilities of the foreign Consuls, in coming to take leave of us, had directed attention to us, for I fancied we became the subject of conversation between two gentlemen, who turned out to be, the one an Italian Prince, a relative of Victor Emmanuel, and the other his French interpreter. The Prince was lame. The interpreter, having ascertained we were returning from the East, soon entered into conversation with us. I felt quite free to relate to him a part of our history, and was near the end of my narrative, when the Captain, to my great mortification, presented himself to ask for our passage-money. No alternative remained but to expose to our new friend the deplorable state of our finances. He immediately had recourse to the Prince, who, with a generosity and a grace which will ever dwell gratefully in my memory, not only satisfied the Captain's demand, but franked us all the way to Paris. I was sorry to see him go on shore at Messina.

Whether the courtesies of the Consuls, or the extreme civilities of the Prince to us, or a knowledge of our misfortunes and adventures—gained through the well-intentioned loquacity of his interpreter—or all these combined, made us special objects of interest, I will not venture to say; but it was impossible to be kinder, more considerate, more deferential than were all on board to us. A

Greek merchant, on his way to Manchester *viâ* Paris, was especially attentive. I refer to him more particularly, because of his kindness at a later period; but the recollection of the courtesies we received on board is, even at this time, most grateful to me. The voyage was, in every respect, one upon which I look back with infinite pleasure.

We arrived at Marseilles at about ten in the morning, and under any other circumstances I should have remained a few days there, to rest, and to deliver my letter of introduction to the French Consul; but circumstanced as we were, the immediate transfer of ourselves to the railway train—notwithstanding we were greatly fatigued—seemed the only prudent course, and we determined to adopt it. Our kind fellow-passenger, the Greek merchant, very courteously invited us to breakfast, which repast pleasantly occupied our attention pretty closely until nearly noon, when we all set out for the railway station, arriving only in time to catch the Paris train.

Our travelling-companions in the same carriage were our Greek friend and a French family, exceedingly courteous, inquisitive, and loquacious. They manifested the deepest interest in so much of our history as I chose to disclose, and I elicited in the course of conversation, that their destination in Paris was the Hôtel du Louvre. I had no notion whatever of the high-class character of this hotel; but upon the face of the assurance that the charges were moderate and the accommodation excellent, and knowing of no other, I passively submitted, upon our arrival in Paris, to follow our new acquaintances to it, and as passively followed the attendant to our apartments; two splendidly appointed bed-rooms on the second floor. An hour or two afterwards, I encountered our Greek friend, who had also taken up his quarters here.

The entry of our names in the hotel register established us at once, as might have been expected, in the category of distinguished foreigners, and our rank and quality, valueless indeed to us, probably impressed the waiters and other attendants with a higher estimate of our monetary resources than was compatible with our real position. Their marked attentions made me, knowing our circumstances, supremely uncomfortable. The very first glimpse of the great court-yard of the hotel had satisfied me that even a brief stay in so grand an establishment would involve me in a financial dilemma the solution of which I did not see, and therefore immediately resolved not to remain one moment longer than would be necessary to provide ourselves with modest furnished **apartments**.

Ayesha was delighted to find herself in so gay a place, and appeared to have not the remotest idea that money could possibly be needed. We were so fatigued after our long journey, that a night's rest, cost what it might, was indispensable; but after breakfast next morning, I and my daughter hurried out in search of a more suitable abode.

We sauntered down the Rue de Rivoli, until we reached a quiet-looking street, into which we turned. It was the Rue du Dauphin. At the very corner we almost ran down a very respectably dressed woman, to whom I apologized for this unintentional collision. She accepted my excuses with smiles, counter-apologies, and assurances of "No harm done, Madame," which encouraged me to inquire whether she knew of any comfortable furnished lodgings in that street, or in the neighbourhood.

"But, yes, Madame," she replied. "Just a few doors down. Would Madame please to inspect them? I am the landlady, Madame, and shall be happy to show you the way."

Nothing could be more fortunate than this, I thought, as we followed our guide, who conducted us to a small-fronted house, at the door of which hung a board, having painted upon it *Maison Meublée. Appartements à louer présentement.*

The "apartments to be let immediately," were clean, nicely furnished, and to our taste; and I soon came to terms, which included board as well as lodging. Rejoicing in my good fortune in so speedily discovering an eligible residence, I returned, much relieved in this respect, to the Hôtel du Louvre; and as I approached it, the consciousness of my inability to discharge my bill smote me with dismay, and set my heart palpitating most violently. But again good fortune favoured me. At the door stood our Greek fellow-traveller. He knew of my penniless condition, and I at once cast myself headlong upon his generosity. He kindly, and without hesitation, ordered my expenses to be included in his own account; and I need scarcely add that, bidding him farewell with grateful thanks—he was leaving that evening for London—I installed myself, without delay, in my new apartments.

CHAPTER IV.

Appeal to M. de Moustier—His envoy—I apply to the Turkish Chargé d'Affaires—Hussein Bey—Arrival in Paris of Mehemet-Djemil Pasha.

IN my destitute position, it was imperative I should lose no time in carrying out my plan of appealing to the French Government; and having taken a few days' rest, I addressed a letter to the Marquis de Moustier, soliciting an audience.

Much to my gratification, and immensely to the astonishment of my landlady, who had assured me I should have to wait at least a fortnight for a reply, I received an answer that same evening, making an appointment for the next day. I was introduced to the Minister's *chef de cabinet* first, who being informed that my business was with his superior, passed me on to another gentleman, whom I recognized as the Marquis's secretary, one of my fellow-travellers on board the *America*, from Constantinople to Piræus. In my letter to the Marquis

I had reminded him of our having made this journey in company.

M. de Moustier received me very courteously, and I related my history, set my position clearly before him, expressed my fears lest my life should be taken, and my daughter forcibly abducted, and finally I appealed for the protection and the interposition of the Government in my behalf. The Marquis listened with the utmost attention, manifesting much sympathy for me and my daughter, and promised to take the matter into consideration, with a view to determine which should be the best way of promoting my object.

I need scarcely say how his promise encouraged and cheered me. I regarded my affair as virtually settled, and returned home to make another as happy as I myself felt. Monsieur and Madame Vacquet, my landlord and my landlady, were equally rejoiced at my success; and upon the strength of it added sundry delicacies to our repast that day. I mention their names, because I desire to record my gratitude to them for their extreme kindness to us during a prolonged period of heavy trial, and because I shall have to speak of them again in connection with circumstances and events of a less agreeable character, with which both were mixed up, though I absolve them of blame, to a very great extent.

My tribulations soon commenced. I retired to rest full of hope, and rose happy the next morning. I and my daughter were already devising our little plans for the future, and revelling in the prospect of independence as well as freedom. We had perhaps soared to impossible heights, but were brought down suddenly to earth by the arrival of a gentleman from the Ministry of Foreign Affairs, in whose very air, and manner, and countenance, I descried indications of an unpleasant mission.

"I have been commissioned to wait upon you, Madame," he said, "to confer with you respecting the subject of your conversation with Monsieur le Marquis de Moustier yesterday. He thought it better to send me than to write to you."

"If what the Marquis has to communicate is of a disagreeable character," I replied, "perhaps it may have been prudent on his part not to commit himself to writing."

"I am entirely in the confidence of M. le Marquis, Madame; and Madame may speak unreservedly to me."

"That, sir, I should do under any circumstances.

Pray may I request to be informed of the nature of your errand?"

The envoy bowed, and resumed.

"Madame, M. le Marquis has very seriously considered your proposition, and before he comes to a final decision as to his own course, thinks it desirable you should be made acquainted with the great difficulties which may impede, or altogether baffle, his attempts to carry out your wishes. This, however, he strongly recommended me to assure you he is most anxious to do."

"Sir, I do not, after the Marquis's protestations of the deep interest he yesterday manifested in our fortunes, call in question the excellence of his intentions. But it is not to re-assure me of these you have come?"

"Assuredly not, Madame. It was to submit a suggestion, of which M. le Marquis may assume all the credit, and which I am to venture to recommend you should seriously consider."

"I will consider, most seriously, any suggestion coming from so friendly a source," I replied, though I felt satisfied now, that this very polite emissary had come with no friendly purpose. "What is it, sir?"

The gentleman seemed somewhat startled by

this direct question. He had recourse for a moment to a highly scented pocket-handkerchief, and then replied in a slightly hesitating manner, as if instinctively aware of the effect his communication would produce upon me.

"Madame, Monsieur le Marquis sees, as I have already intimated, great difficulties in the way of successfully prosecuting your claims; and having reason to believe that you and your daughter would not be molested in Constantinople, and that you would have immense advantages, were you to seek on the spot the redress to which you are so justly entitled, M. le Marquis would urgently recommend——"

"That I and my daughter should return to Constantinople!" I exclaimed, ere he had time to complete the sentence.

"Precisely," responded the gentleman, with an inclination of the head. "Madame has admirably seized the suggestion of M. le Marquis."

I started to my feet, indignant and astounded.

"Sir," I said, perhaps with less prudence than bluntness and show of anger, "M. le Marquis might have spared himself the trouble of sending you upon such an errand. We quitted Turkey because our lives were not safe. We quitted it with the firm determination never to return, and return to that country we never will, unless by force."

Turning to my daughter, I communicated the substance of this conversation, and the Marquis de Moustier's suggestion, during which time the perfumed pocket-handkerchief was again brought into active service.

"I would rather die than go back to Constantinople," exclaimed Ayesha; and she burst into tears.

"You hear, sir?" I said to our visitor. "My daughter declares she prefers death to replacing herself in the power of her father. We are both of the same mind. You can convey this, as our reply, to Monsieur le Marquis."

"I shall, of course, relate to Monsieur de Moustier what has occurred," replied the envoy; "but Madame will do well to reflect. Madame's position is very critical. How will Madame live, without resources, in a city like Paris? It is true, Mademoiselle's superb beauty may serve her in lieu of a dowry, but without a dowry, it is rare for a young girl, however beautiful, to meet with an eligible husband. Any other alternative is really too terrible even to think of."

My blood boiled; and I now wonder how I

controlled myself. I translated the gentleman's speech to Ayesha, who, with flashing eyes, retorted:

"Rather than marry a Turk, I would become even the mistress of an European."

I communicated to the Marquis's messenger what my daughter had said. He slightly inclined his head, and resumed:

"I have not ended, Madame," he said. "Monsieur le Marquis desired me to state, that if Madame has quite decided not to adopt his suggestion—made entirely in Madame's interests—he should not feel himself at liberty to urge his views, but would place himself entirely at Madame's disposal. Madame would, in such an event, have the kindness to deposit in his Excellency's hands the papers and documents indispensable to the establishment and the prosecution of Madame's claims, and Monsieur le Marquis will use his utmost efforts to recover Madame's property."

This sounded fair enough, but the Marquis's proposition struck me as so singular, acquainted as he was with our history and our position, that my suspicions of his sincerity were aroused. I therefore dismissed our visitor with an intimation that I would await the result of his report to his Excellency, and in the meantime collect my papers ready to be delivered to him at a moment's notice.

The gentleman bowed himself nearly double, and took his departure, scattering around him an atmosphere of musk, attar of roses, and mille-fleurs. He never honoured us with a second call.

In order to discharge any further claim M. de Moustier may be thought to have upon the reader's attention, in connection with my affairs, I am compelled here to forestall events.

His Excellency, no doubt influenced, as I must now believe, by confidential intimations from the Turkish Embassy, observed silence towards me, notwithstanding his stout professions of interest in us, and his formal promise to aid me in obtaining either my property or an annual income from my husband. I waited several weeks, in expectation of a communication from him. As none came, I addressed him a second time. The reply, curt, formal, and cold as officialism gone down to freezing point, was to the effect that his Excellency could not interfere; but, if I would see the Turkish Chargé d'Affaires, they would both confer, and determine whether anything and what could be done in my case.

This was decisive. No help could be expected from this quarter, and I gave up M. de Moustier with feelings easy to imagine, but which I do not care to describe.

I cannot say the result of my overtures wholly disappointed me, or took me by surprise. In the interval between my two letters, I had paid a visit to the Turkish official referred to, to solicit an advance of money. He informed me that my husband, on receiving intelligence of my arrival in Paris, with our daughter, had immediately telegraphed to the Embassy, prohibiting the advance to us of a single penny.

No wonder M. de Moustier's sympathy had cooled down so rapidly.

I do not now entertain the remotest doubt that my husband—who, as I subsequently learnt, had telegraphed to the officials at the Turkish Legation the fact of my flight from Constantinople—received through them, and through the same rapid medium, intelligence of our presence in Paris, as soon as the circumstance became known; and I am not by any means certain M. de Moustier was not privy to that communication. Within a day of our arrival, and for the space of nearly a fortnight after it, the newspapers devoted to us long notices and leading articles, elaborately embroidered, and we thus became, innocently enough, the authors as well as the victims of a ten days' sensation. For the intelligence to reach Constantinople, in the ordinary course, would have required several days, and none but the official parasites at the Ottoman Embassy, or a personage like M. de Moustier, anxious to stand well with all parties, could have the slightest interest in forwarding to Constantinople special information concerning two poor fugitive women, whose capture and consignment into the hands of their persecutors could, after all, only promote private revenge. Unfortunately, diplomacy does not despise unworthy means to achieve an object, and Turkish policy knows no obstacle, and ignores all morality.

During the interval referred to, and in the midst of my trouble and anxiety, I received one morning a call from Hussein Bey. On his mother's side, Hussein was related to Mustapha Pasha, son of the late Mehemet Ali, the famous Viceroy of Egypt. His visit had a friendly object, I must believe, for after inquiring into our position, he proffered me pecuniary help. At that moment, I yet had hopes of obtaining my own through M. de Moustier, and my pride also prevented me from accepting assistance from the Bey. Soon after he paid us a second visit, and then strongly recommended us to return to Constantinople. This suggestion confirmed me in my determination not to lay myself under obligation to him. Everything that savoured of Constantinople excited my suspicions, and aroused my alarm.

I had, as will probably be remembered, a letter for the Emperor's Chamberlain, Count de Flahaut, which the French Consul at Athens had given to me, and also one to his wife. He was one of the protégés of this high personage, over whom the lady exercised considerable influence. She had accompanied her husband to Athens, to induct him into his consulate, but had shortly after returned to Paris, to be near the patron of her husband, whose promotion she was anxious to secure. I took the earliest opportunity of calling upon this lady, Ayesha accompanying me.

We were received with great civility, but I noticed that Madame seemed strangely impressed by Ayesha's appearance. She gazed at my daughter with a singular air of curiosity and interest, scarcely moving her eyes from her for several seconds, and every now and then renewing her stare. Our conversation soon fell upon the subject of the letter to the Chamberlain, which, it appeared, her husband had not referred to. I fancied I perceived an expression like dissatisfaction come over her face, upon my soliciting the favour of her advice how I should proceed, as I supposed so exalted an officer of the Imperial household was not easy of access. She confirmed me in this view, dwelling, as I thought unduly, upon the claims his duties made upon his time, but offering to manage an audience for me at the earliest possible moment. I was somewhat startled, however, and not a little amused, when presently, drawing me aside, she cautioned me against taking Ayesha with me.

"The Count, you see," she said, in the most confidential of under-tones, "has the reputation of being a great gallant; and those eyes of your daughter's, her Oriental style, her *tout-ensemble*, are so striking, that I really—I cannot say such would be the case—but—I would advise you. Ha—hem! You know, there are so many facilities in Paris for —for—well—the fact is, your daughter is very beautiful, and His Excellency the Chamberlain is over-impressionable."

A certain green eye winked at me in the most persistent, provoking manner whilst Madame, hemming and ha-ing, was relieving her mind of the burden that oppressed it. I thanked her for her excellent and friendly caution, which I assured her should not be thrown away, and we took leave of her, receiving a renewal of her promise to promote an early interview with her husband's patron.

Some days having elapsed without my receiving any intimation of an appointment, I paid her a second visit, and was assured of Madame's regret that up to that moment she had not had the opportunity of fulfilling her promise, but she would not neglect it. I should hear from her without fail.

But the days passed and nothing came, and as I had acquired sufficient experience of Monsieur le Marquis de Moustier's policy, I did not anticipate better success at the hands of the Chamberlain, so I renounced any further attempt to present him the Consul's letter.

We had been in Paris a month; my hopes in M. le Moustier had vanished; I had learnt, to my cost, that my husband and his people were active in their machinations to get me and my girl once more into their power. I had no friends, no money, and was living upon strangers, whose means of existence were precarious, and whom I could not expect would trust me indefinitely. I was supremely wretched; my sole pleasure being the intense delight of my daughter in the sights and gaiety of the city. One day M. Vacquet brought me intelligence of the arrival of Mehemet Djemil Pacha, Ambassador from the Porte. I did not then ask myself how my worthy landlord came to know so soon, and before the newspapers had recorded the fact, that this dignitary was in Paris. I was not then aware he paid almost daily visits to the Embassy; but his news inspired me with renewed hopes, and I despatched a note to the Ambassador soliciting an advance of money, stating my position, and requesting his interference in my affairs.

His Excellency's reply reached me in due course, and without over-much delay. It was brief, but decided. His instructions were imperative, not to afford us any assistance whatsoever; but if we would return to Constantinople, he would discharge all claims against us in Paris, and defray our expenses back to the Turkish capital. It was about this time I received the last communication from M. de Moustier, as already stated. The two answers left me in no doubt as to my husband's purpose. I was to be starved into submission. What under such terrible circumstances could I do? Await events! This was my decision.

CHAPTER V.

Visitors from the Pope—The Abbé Boré—My landlord and the Turkish Embassy—I escape a snare.

In the East we are believers in Destiny. That to which a man is born he will come to. If there be no such thing as Fate, it is difficult, impossible indeed, to account for the vicissitudes which befall some, and others wholly escape. The end comes through a concatenation of minor events, of which we appreciate the importance only when the consummation is reached. The special Providence in the fall of a sparrow, which Christianity inculcates, is but another form of asserting Destiny, and the belief in it is embodied in more than one proverb in all the nations I have visited. I invite those who call this theory in question to follow up the incidents of my life, and mark how, wholly independently of my will, the force of circumstances has ruled my fate.

But I must not digress into philosophy.

We had been in our new lodgings about three weeks or a month, when, one day, on our return from a walk, our landlady informed us that two ladies, dressed in black, had called during our absence, and left a message to the effect that they would pay us a visit next morning. Their names they did not give. Speculation respecting these new visitors kept us both awake the early part of the night. We were up betimes in the morning, and duly prepared ourselves to receive them, full of anxious anticipation of the object of their call.

At last they arrived. They were announced as Madame la Princesse Davidoff, and Mademoiselle de Monroi, and had called in consequence of a communication from the Pope, who felt a deep interest in us: in my daughter especially. His Holiness had heard of our arrival in Paris through my sister-in-law, and of my intention to make Ayesha a Roman Catholic, if she desired to become one. He had therefore written to Monsieur de Monroi, Mademoiselle's father: hence the visit of these ladies.

I must here remind the reader that my mother-in-law and my sister-in-law, originally Protestants, had been converted to Catholicism in Rome under the immediate auspices of the Holy Father, and that Monsieur de Monroi was his private agent in Paris; religious, political, fanatical, and financial.

Of course we could not be otherwise than flattered by such a mark of interest from such a quarter, and by the condescension of these ladies in paying us so friendly a visit. Thus much I intimated, expressing a hope that it would lead to more intimate intercourse. Then followed our history, an exposition of our actual condition, of our plans, of our apprehensions, and our hopes.

The ladies became more and more moved as I proceeded to narrate the sufferings of myself and my daughter. What a truly romantic tale! What a pretty Oriental name was Ayesha! How interesting to learn she felt so anxious to abjure the religion of her pagan ancestors, and to embrace Christianity! They would be, oh! so glad to become her instructors in the fundamental principles of their own faith! So interesting, too! a convert direct from the superstition invented by Mahomet! And we really were rich, and we had diamonds and other valuable jewelry in Constantinople, and estates, all our own, and to recover possession of which we sought the kindly offices of the French Government! How pleased they would be if they could only help us! —and so on.

Probably from motives of extreme delicacy these ladies did not offer us the only help we most and so sorely needed at that moment, and which I should so gratefully have accepted. I, too, actuated by similar motives—perhaps mistaken ones in my deplorable position,—dared not venture to solicit pecuniary aid. Before they left, it was agreed they should come thrice or oftener every week to teach Ayesha French, and impart to her the religious instruction preliminary and indispensable to her embracing, in due form, the Christian faith. I also felt that their influence might be a protection in the event of our persecutors seeking to obtain our forcible expulsion : a contingency I had good reason for believing not improbable. Moreover, and wholly apart from any selfish considerations, I felt drawn towards them.

Some few days after, I received a visit from another lady, the Countess de Bac, sister of Prince Davidoff. I recognised her as a frequent visitor at Madame Vacquet's. The Countess's interest in her arose, as I afterwards learnt, out of an accident to the Count, who was one day taken suddenly ill in the street, and accommodated in my landlady's house until he felt able to return home, which he did in a few hours. This incident had no more than a momentary interest for me when I heard it narrated, but, strange to say, proved of greater importance to my fortunes than it could ever have entered into my mind to anticipate.

It was my custom to walk out every day with my daughter and Djehad. We always conversed in Turkish, for the simple reason that Ayesha knew no other language. One day—a short time after the call of the Princess Davidoff and Mademoiselle de Monroi—we passed a gentleman, who, hearing us talk in this uncommon tongue, looked earnestly at us, then turned and followed us. Presently he overtook us, and, addressing me, apologised for the liberty. He had overheard us converse in a tongue familiar to him, though unusual to be heard in the streets of Paris; his interest and curiosity had been excited, and he had ventured to approach us. He spoke to me in Turkish.

The stranger's manners were remarkably courteous, and his grave aspect and benevolent expression of countenance impressed me most favourably. There was also something of the ecclesiastic in his style of dress, and this gave me a little additional confidence that he was at least no common man seeking to thrust himself into our company.

Still walking by my side, he informed me that he had laboured in the East for twenty-five years, in the capacity of a Roman Catholic missionary priest, and had not long returned thence. He belonged to the religious Order of Lazarists, and his name was Boré—the Abbé Boré. He begged to be permitted to conduct us home, and to call upon us in a few days.

In answer to this confidential communication, I gave him to understand that, although we were shy of making new acquaintances, and had strong reasons for remaining in obscurity, his position and his profession decided me to agree to his proposal. I then disclosed my name, on hearing which he manifested a little surprise, it being quite familiar to him. His interest in us increased when he heard that the Princess Davidoff and Mademoiselle de Monroi had visited us. He knew them both, intimately, and seemed delighted to learn that Ayesha desired to renounce Mahometanism for the Christian faith; and for my part I felt equally pleased that Fate had thrown us across the path of a man so pre-eminently qualified to assist in preparing my daughter to receive the new revelation. Under the circumstances, the circle was the very best into which my daughter could have been introduced. The opening was equally desirable from many other points of view.

I had lived upon the Vacquets for a prolonged period without any hopeful indication of a change for the better in my position. I often marvelled at the extreme forbearance of these people, and my gratitude knew no bounds. At the same time, it gradually became to me a source of uneasiness to find how well M. Vacquet seemed acquainted with everything that was passing at the Ottoman Embassy. This uneasiness, at first vague and slight, increased as time rolled on, and I began at last to ask myself whether I had any reasonable grounds for it.

Upon this point my mind was not yet made up, when, one morning, Madame Vacquet presented herself, and, after considerable circumlocution, intimated that her husband desired a settlement of his account. This demand—though not entirely unexpected—coming in so peremptory a manner, and notwithstanding my host's full knowledge of my straitened circumstances, somewhat startled me. I reminded Madame Vacquet that I had concealed nothing from her; that she knew I could only await the result of the steps then being taken by my new friends to obtain my property, and assistance from Constantinople; that I felt myself under great obligations to her, to which I begged her to add the greater one of waiting a little longer. Madame left me with dissatisfaction depicted upon her countenance, and giving me to understand that there was a limit to waiting.

She renewed her application the next day, the next after, and the next, always with the same result, but daily becoming more pressing. At last Monsieur Vacquet himself came, and receiving still the same reply, told me if I did not pay him, he should find a means of compelling me to do so. Thus threatened, my indignation was aroused, and a violent scene ensued, which suddenly terminated by the rapid disappearance of Monsieur Vacquet as a lady in black quietly entered the room. It was the Countess de Bac.

As a matter of course, the Countess immediately inquired into the cause of my discomposure.

"My dear Madame," I said, "it is simply a question of money. I owe Monsieur Vacquet a considerable sum, and cannot pay him until my affairs are either settled or in a fair way of being so. These people have been very lenient to me, and it is only within the last few days that they have pressed me for payment. In fact, their importunity has become a daily persecution. I am certain there must be some secret cause for this change. I am almost in despair, for my prospects seem darker than ever."

The Countess listened to my explanation, but as I drew near the end her countenance lost its habitual serenity. She had not yet taken a seat. Crossing the apartment, she seized the bell-pull and gave it a sharp tug. In a few minutes Madame Vacquet answered the summons.

"I wish to speak to Monsieur, your husband," said the Countess. "Send him up."

Madame Vacquet, taken aback by the Countess's peremptory manner, coloured up, coughed a very little cough, and inquired, hesitatingly, if she herself would not do equally well.

"No!" was the reply. "I must see Monsieur."

Monsieur could not have been far from the door, for scarcely had Madame vanished than he appeared, and evidently considerably disconcerted.

"Monsieur Vacquet," said the Countess, with a severity of tone and a manner I did not understand, "what is this I hear from Madame la Princesse de Kibrizli? What is the meaning of this persecution of her?"

I noticed that Monsieur Vacquet appeared even more discomposed by this apostrophe than when he came in. With an effort at calmness, which was not entirely successful, he replied:

"Madame la Comtesse will excuse me, but it is only natural we should seek to be paid. We are only poor people. We have not the means of giving long credit, and—and we have not yet seen the colour of money from—from—Madame—la—Princesse."

The speaker laid special emphasis upon the title the Countess had invested me with, but if by his deliberate mode of repeating it he intended to convey a sarcasm, any momentary gratification that slender piece of malice may have given him was dearly purchased.

"I cannot blame you for seeking what is your due," retorted the Countess; "but under the circumstances, knowing Madame's position, and permit me to add, knowing that we are her friends—her friends, Monsieur Vacquet—your mode of proceeding has no excuse. It is shameful—it is abominable—it is——"

"But, Madame la Comtesse," he exclaimed, now white and trembling with mortification, "we are pressed for money—we are so poor——"

"I know that," replied the Countess, interrupting in her turn. "I knew you were poor when you besought me to lend you five thousand francs, not so long since. I have never troubled you for them."

"That is true," said Monsieur Vacquet, bowing. "Madame la Comtesse has been very generous and kind, and we are very grateful to Madame."

"Then how can you have the conscience—how dare you to persecute my friend here," resumed the Countess, "when you know it is out of her power at present to pay you? What is the amount of your bill?"

"Three thousand five hundred francs, Madame la Comtesse," answered he.

"Very well," she retorted. "You will at once hand Madame a receipt for that sum, in full discharge of all your claims upon her, and you will have the goodness to send me the balance in—in— I will give you a fortnight. You will please understand that my request is peremptory."

"But, Madame la Comtesse," remonstrated Monsieur Vacquet, "allow me to explain."

"Leave the room, sir," exclaimed the Countess, with an imperious motion of the hand. "There is nothing to explain. Leave the room! I wish to be alone with Madame."

My worthy landlord withdrew entirely crestfallen, and without venturing a word in resentment of sundry strong appellations showered upon him by my indignant friend. I felt sorry for the man, for, after all, I thought, I am his debtor, and without immediate prospect of paying him.

For my own part, I could not find a word to utter, so confounded and overcome was I by such an act of generosity, and so unexpected a release from an embarrassment of such magnitude. Before the Countess left, I recovered my equanimity, and thanked her for her munificent interposition on my behalf at this serious crisis.

"Do not say anything more, my dear," she observed; "but we must remove you at once to less expensive quarters. You must not renew your obligations to these rogues."

I thought the term somewhat exaggerated, but soon had reason to consider it mild. The Countess had not long quitted the apartment, before Monsieur and Madame Vacquet again entered it, contrition and penitence depicted upon their countenance, obsequiousness and humility in their tone and manner.

"Pardon, Madame," said the lady, assuming the office of speaker, "a thousand pardons; but we owe you an explanation."

"I do not require any," I replied. "You are paid. I shall leave your house. That is enough."

"Madame," continued my landlady, "can at least listen to what we have to say. It is only right Madame should know what has passed. It is Madame's interest to know."

This appeal struck me as singular. A sudden light seemed to be breaking upon me. My curiosity was excited. I intimated my readiness to listen.

"Madame," resumed Madame Vacquet, "it was my husband who insisted upon my pressing for the money. This is the truth which I am telling you."

"Yes, Madame," interposed the husband. "It is the truth; but I was urged to do so."

I manifested the astonishment I felt.

"By whom, pray?" I asked.

"Why, Madame, who should do such a thing if not the people at the Turkish Embassy? Yes, Madame, they are bad people," was his reply.

"And you were in league with them—with my enemies," I retorted; "and all this time?"

"No, Madame! Pardon! Not in league with Madame's enemies," exclaimed Madame Vacquet, taking up the cudgels in defence of her husband.

"How, then," I asked, "came he to obey instructions from such a quarter?"

"The thing is very simple, Madame," he resumed. "It was natural, as we were giving credit to Madame, that we should take an interest in Madame's affairs, and that I should go, from time to time, to the Ottoman Embassy. One day that I was there, I was invited to speak with his Excellency, who asked me many questions, and if Madame was paying me. What could I say, Madame, but no? But I assured him we had full confidence in Madame."

"That is true, too," interjected Madame Vacquet.

"What then?" I asked.

"His Excellency shook his head," answered the estimable Monsieur Vacquet, " and said I must not go too far. It was very doubtful whether Madame would ever receive anything from Constantinople. 'Then, I said, 'but, Excellency, how am I to get paid?'"

"Naturally," exclaimed Madame Vacquet, again.

"'Monsieur Vacquet,' said his Excellency," continued that worthy gentleman, "'your bill must, of course, be paid; but it is too small as yet.' Observe, Madame, I did not tell him till he asked me the amount. 'You must let it run on until it reaches a larger sum; perhaps—well, say three thousand five hundred or four thousand francs. Madame will not be able to pay it, nor is it probable she will find any one ready to lend her so large a sum. You will then press her for the money, and at the last you will go to the police, who will come to me. I will manage that. Then the police will arrest these people, and place them in my hands, and when that is done, I will pay your bill and any other expenses.' This, Madame, is the exact truth; and Madame will see that, under the circumstances, this seemed to be our only way to get paid."

"But," here again interposed the irrepressible Madame Vacquet, "Madame can remain here as long as she pleases. We shall not trouble her again for payment; no, Madame, be sure of that! We have confidence in Madame."

If I had given way to my first impulse on learning the part my host had played in the despicable plot against me, which circumstances, and a desire to justify himself, had alone led him to disclose, I should have ordered him and his wife out of my sight. But the remembrance of their kindness, without which I and my children must have starved, predominated over my resentment. I could see that their moral perception was too obtuse to permit them to perceive how, in their desire to secure their own interests, they had made themselves parties to a gross act of treachery, which but for a mere accident might have led to the most disastrous results, so far as myself and my daughter, and Djehad were concerned. On the other hand, I felt that their kindness had not the merit of spontaneity, although it had been none the less so to me in effect; so gratitude carried the day.

"Monsieur," I said, "if you can reconcile your course with your conscience, well and good. Your ideas of right differ from mine. I will not reproach you for having acted towards me with such duplicity. I shall always be grateful for the service you have rendered me in giving us shelter and food when we had not the means of procuring either; but what you have divulged to me of your relations with the officials of the Ottoman Embassy has destroyed my confidence in your good faith. It has also aroused my alarm for our safety, and I am convinced that the sooner we are out of your house the better."

"If Madame would only put us to the proof," exclaimed Madame Vacquet.

I interrupted her by stating that my determination was not to be changed; and she and her husband retired, protesting that their intentions had never been other than kind, and that circumstances alone had given them a different complexion. No sooner were they gone, than I hastened to communicate to the Countess and to the Princess Davidoff what had transpired, beseeching them to **procure** apartments for us without delay.

That same evening **we** were fetched **away, and** conducted to another private hotel on the other side of the water, in which we remained a couple **of** days. By this time a small but comfortable suite **of** apartments was provided for us, **and we hastened to** take possession of them, the Countess and **her** friends guaranteeing our expenses for a period of three months, which we hoped would be the extreme limit the settlement of my affairs would require.

CHAPTER VI.

Ayesha's instruction in religious matters—Her notions of the Christian faith—Her baptism—The Ottoman Embassy still at work.

OUR new residence was in the Rue de Vaugirard, Faubourg St. Germain, the Belgravia of Paris. In this quarter the old legitimate aristocracy, the *ancienne noblesse* of France, delight. It is redolent of exclusiveness, the legitimist element, and devotecism. In its saloons and in its households the grand manners of the olden time still retain their ascendancy. Convents and religious establishments abound in it, and the tiara and the *fleur-de-lys* receive an almost equal amount of homage. Into its select circles we were most graciously admitted through the Countess de Bac and her friends. Our name and misfortunes were the current topic of conversation; and wherever we went, groups clustered about us. At the dinner-tables and receptions of my new friends, I met with many grand personages; but as I am writing a simple history of my own personal experiences and vicissitudes, any record of what I saw and noted whilst mixing with the great folks in Paris would be out of place.

The ladies I have specially mentioned, a few of their more intimate acquaintances, and the Abbé Boré, were now our constant visitors. They were most assiduous in their endeavours to teach my daughter French, and to prepare her for the great event in her life which was to sever her thenceforward from all sympathy on the part of her countrymen; nay, more, which was to stamp her, in their estimation, as a giaour, a renegade, meriting death at the hands of the first true follower of Mahomet who might choose to take her life, and thereby gain a palace of diamond in Paradise.

Ayesha's renunciation of her ancestral faith was certain to excite an unprecedented sensation at Constantinople, and to drive her father and his fanatical connections to the last degree of fury. Why, it is necessary to explain.

Kibrizli, my husband, was a descendant of the Prophet's, and amongst the strictest observers of Mahomet's law. He was entitled—in virtue of his descent—to wear the green, the Prophet's colour, and for the same reason, so too was our daughter Ayesha, who had even received the name of the Prophet's favourite wife. That any Turk should abjure Mahometanism is, under any circumstances, a crime; but that one of the sacred race of the Prophet should turn infidel and embrace Christianity, was a crime double-dyed and unpardonable, deserving ignominy and death in this world, and certain to be visited with exclusion from Paradise in the other. The baptism of Ayesha would be regarded as a dishonour to her, as well as a disgrace to her father, and her association with European fanatics only aggravated the insult, and crowned the dishonour. If my husband sought revenge only in consequence of my escape with our daughter, religious fanaticism would now intensify his hatred, and we might expect persecution even unto death, and that no means would be neglected to inveigle us once more into his power. I entertained no doubt whatever that at this very moment we were closely watched by spies, and the course of this narrative will prove that our escape with life from their toils, up to this time, was nothing short of miraculous. Although I had reason to suspect that my husband was early made aware of my daughter's purpose to embrace Christianity, not until later did I ascertain this to be actually the fact.

I must conclude that when Ayesha had learnt to answer the questions relating to the fundamental principles of the faith of which the Abbé was undeniably so sincere and eminent an apostle, he felt satisfied she had become a very good Christian, and to complete her character as such, needed only to be formally made a member of the Roman Catholic Church. So, at last, the day was fixed for the ceremony of her baptism to be celebrated.

During the period which I may call Ayesha's novitiate, she was an object of special interest to her spiritual teachers. Brought up in the seclusion of the Harem, in the densest ignorance; surrounded by influences of the most demoralizing and debasing kind; having no ideas of morality save those taught in the Koran; fanatically attached to the creed founded by her ancestor; regarding men as the absolute masters of creation, and women as mere creatures born to be subject to them in all things; her instructors were as surprised to find her such a child in experience, as she was herself astonished to discover, that as a woman, she had a value in this world, that as a member of the human family, she had in God a common Father, in Christ a common Saviour, and in Heaven a.

common inheritance. This was to her the new revelation.

But although her mind was as yet a blank with respect to acquired knowledge of men and things, its natural acuteness often led her to put to her instructors questions which it severely taxed their ingenuity to answer. As a rule I was present at what were called her lessons, and many of the conversations between the Abbé Boré and her are still fresh in my memory. I do not know that I can recall them in anything like order, but a few specimens may be interesting, as illustrating the train of thought the new teaching awakened in her.

AYESHA. "Yes! I understand that the Christian's God is a spirit. So is the God of Mahomet. But I cannot understand what a spirit is."

The ABBÉ. "Can you not accept the God of the Christian and the God of Mahomet as one and the same Being?"

AYESHA. "Certainly. But that does not teach me what a spirit is, and therefore I cannot understand God."

The ABBÉ. "Did your Mahometan instructors teach you what a spirit is?"

AYESHA. "No!"

The ABBÉ. "Yet you believed in the God of Mahomet, as a spirit, without understanding Him."

AYESHA. "Yes! But I thought Christianity would explain this; and I want to know what God is like."

The ABBÉ. "My child, as no one has ever seen God, no one can tell what he is like. Did you believe in the God of Mahomet?"

"AYESHA. "Oh, assuredly. The Koran enjoins us to do so."

The ABBÉ. "Well, the Bible is now your Koran, and you must believe it as you believed the Koran. You accepted in faith the teaching of the one, you must now equally accept in faith the teaching of the other."

AYESHA. "I do, Abbé; but I do not understand why I did believe the Koran, any more than why I now believe the Bible. I was told I must believe it; everybody about me did so, and in this way I came to do the same. For us, then, the Christians were infidels. Now, I am told that all who do not believe in the Bible are infidels, and I find that I must believe in it, because all Christians do so! It is, then, only a change of name, the Bible for the Koran."

This was in the earlier time. It will be observed, that at this period she accepted the Bible as a simple matter of course, because she was told she must do so, as a Christian; and that it was not from any conviction of its superior authority to the Koran. But she was greatly struck with the higher morality taught by the Saviour, whose life she greatly admired.

Here is what passed on another occasion.

The ABBÉ. "My child, the carpenter's son was not a prophet, as Mahomet professed to be, but the true and only Son of God; Son of the Virgin Mary who conceived Him by the mysterious operation of the Holy Ghost."

AYESHA. "It is much more difficult to believe this, Abbé, than that Christ was a great Prophet, far greater than Mahomet. In fact, I do not comprehend it at all. If God was his Father, I cannot understand what the Holy Ghost had to do in the matter; nor how Mary could have remained a virgin and become a mother."

The ABBÉ. "This, my dear child, is one of those mysteries which our Holy Church requires all her children to accept, in faith, upon the testimony of the Scriptures, upon the traditions handed down to her, direct from the Apostles, and upon her authority. These are things not to be understood, not to be inquired into, but simply to be accepted."

AYESHA. "But, Abbé, all this is so new to me, that I am startled, and cannot help asking myself if it can be true. I desire to believe what you tell me, but sometimes I feel that I never shall be able to do so."

The ABBÉ. "Misgivings will afflict and trouble you, my child, until you are favoured with light from above. You must pray earnestly to God—ours and Mahomet's—and He will enlighten you, and give you courage to resist the promptings of the great enemy of mankind, who is seeking to snatch your soul from Him by inspiring you with doubt and unbelief. It ought not to be more difficult for you to accept in faith the mystery of the Holy Incarnation, than it was for you to believe in Mahomet's journey to the Seventh Heaven, mounted upon the back of the Borak."

On other occasions the life and the character of Jesus Christ, as compared with Mahomet's, became the topics of conversation. This was in the later time, when her mind seemed at last to grasp the sublimity of the Scriptural revelation. Nevertheless, I could trace in her remarks a lingering remnant of the old superstition: such was the force of early education and habit.

"I must believe," she said one day to the Abbé, "that Christ was greater than Mahomet, because he was better. But the Christians call Mahomet an impostor, because he declared he had been chosen by God as his Prophet, just as Christ announced that he had been sent by God to redeem mankind. Mahomet may have told the truth."

The ABBÉ. "The religion he taught, my child, his mode of life, his sanguinary career, all forbid the conclusion that he held any mission from God. Christ taught love for hatred, good for evil, absolute purity of life, and practised what he taught; and at last gave up his own life to redeem humanity at large from the consequences of sin."

AYESHA. "I know I am bound to accept in faith what all Christians are taught to believe is the truth. When I was a Mahometan I believed everything the Koran said, and I did not seek to investigate the mysteries of our religion, nor to satisfy myself whether the Prophet was or was not what he announced himself to be. I took for granted whatever I was taught. But now I am converted, it is not so. I can see that the Bible is a better book than the Koran, that Christ was divinely pure and good, and that the religion He taught is purer than that of Mahomet's. Still, for all that, and notwithstanding my desire to believe everything you tell me, Abbé, I cannot avoid asking myself why the penalty our first parents incurred by their sin should be visited upon all their descendants, and have necessitated the self-sacrifice of Christ. To punish the innocent for the sin of their ancestors, seems to me to be a gross injustice; and if Christ is the Son of God, why did he allow himself to be put to death? He had only to exercise his power, and he might have saved himself."

The ABBÉ. "My child, the Jews challenged Jesus to come down from the Cross, if he was the Son of God, and they would then believe in Him. It is not for us to conjecture why He did not give evidence of His power in the way His enemies wished; nor ought we to challenge the infinite justice of God, by attempting to measure it according to our finite standard. Rest satisfied that what now seems dark to us poor unworthy mortals, will one day be made clear. Our duty is to have faith, and to accept implicitly as truth whatever our Holy Mother the Church teaches."

In this spirit Ayesha was prepared for her

entrance into the Church, and I saw the day for the ceremony of her baptism draw near with feelings of intense satisfaction.

The Countess de Bac had promised to stand as her godmother; but, for some reason I did not then know, some few days before the day of the ceremony she suddenly declined, without giving any other explanation than that her brother the Prince would not allow her to carry out her wish. She was therefore replaced by the Princess Soukolska, a Polish lady.

The ceremony took place on the 8th May, 1867, in a chapel attached to the Convent of Convalescent Children; a kind of infirmary, supported by voluntary contributions, and in maintaining which our kind patronesses were interested. It is situated in the Rue de Sèvres, and this chapel was selected because it was not open to promiscuous worshippers. Besides, it was thought advisable to keep the affair as quiet as possible.

At two o'clock, the invited party—which included the Countess de Bac, the Marchioness de Strada and her two daughters, Princess Davidoff, Mademoiselle de Monroi, and a few other ladies—assembled in the little sanctuary referred to, Ayesha being attended to the altar by her godmother and myself. The chapel had been very prettily decorated for the occasion by the Sisters of Charity attached to the establishment, and it presented a most charming appearance.

Our excellent friend, the Abbé Boré, officiated. Ayesha was attired in the simplest manner; a dress of white muslin and a tulle veil of the same colour, with no other ornament than her rich black hair. It set off, to the best advantage, her Oriental type of beauty, her lustrous black eyes and white skin. Her expressive countenance beamed with contentment as she walked up the aisle to the communion rails; and throughout the ceremony she preserved a quiet demeanour and the same happy expression. When the Abbé Boré, giving her the name of Maria Isabella, poured the holy water on her head—in the midst of the most religious silence—a marked sensation was visible in all present. It was the gathering of another lamb into the fold, and they were the gentle shepherds who had saved it.

As for myself, tears of joy I could not restrain, ran down my face, and I could only feebly and in my inmost heart thank Almighty God that my child whom I so tenderly loved, for whom I had more than once risked my life, for whom I had sacrificed country, wealth,—all, had been rescued from Heathendom and brought to know the Truth, and the ineffable blessing of the Redeemer's love.

As soon as the ceremony was over, my daughter was embraced by all her friends present, and received their congratulations. We then adjourned with them to the Princess Davidoff's, where we sat down to a splendid lunch the Princess had generously provided in honour of the event.

That day is one of the red-letter days in my life's calendar. It was clouded by only one disturbing thought. The Countess de Bac had taken the same deep interest in the ceremony as though she had retained her original position as my daughter's godmother. I had no reason to complain of the substitution in her place of the Princess Soukolska, at the last moment, nor to question the validity of the reason alleged for the change; nevertheless the incident troubled me. What reasons had Prince Davidoff for disapproving of his sister's intention?

The mystery was cleared up within two or three days.

I had occasion to call upon the Countess' dressmaker, who—almost as a matter of course—began to comment upon the recent ceremony. She retained a vivid remembrance of everybody, and after the fashion of high-class **gossips, had much to** say about every one of her grand customers. I am constrained to add, **in justice** to her, that she retailed no scandal.

My turn **came in due course.** She very much pitied Madame—alluding to me. Madame and **her** daughter had suffered so **much! What a horror that** Madame's enemies **could not leave** her alone, now Madame was so far away from them! What object had they in calumniating **Madame** and her daughter?

I began to get interested.

Madame was so good and kind, and Mademoiselle so condescending, **so *naïve*, so** beautiful; for though she *was* married, **a marriage** in Turkey did not count; and she had **a right to run away** from her husband if she **chose, and might consider** herself a *demoiselle* all the same.

"Oh! Here is our **history,"** thought I, "and something **more."**

She was sure Madame la Comtesse de Bac did not believe a word **of the** reports to the detriment of Madame—that was. me—and her daughter, which had reached her brother; **but men were so ungenerous, and made no allowances for** poor weak women placed in delicate **and difficult** positions. It was **quite certain that** but for these **reports,** Madame de

Bac would have stood godmother to Mademoiselle, as she had signified her intention of doing. Those people in Constantinople and at the Ottoman Embassy must be the very worst of created human beings, or they would not strive so hard to undermine Madame in the estimation of her friends! Oh, dear no! Madame de Bac would never have condescended to say a word to her—the speaker—of these things; but Madame la Comtesse's maid knew all her secrets, "and I, Madame," she added, "work for her, as well as for Madame la Comtesse; so, of course," &c., &c.

Here was the murder out! My husband and his *entourage* had set afloat calumniating reports of us, with a view to damage us in the estimation of our new friends. They had reached the Countess' brother, and he—probably without wholly believing them—had nevertheless been so far influenced by them as to dissuade his sister from undertaking the office of godmother to my daughter.

I never disclosed to the Countess what I had heard; but my eyes were now fully open to the snares that were being laid for us.

CHAPTER VII.

I renew my appeals to my husband—The Sultan's visit to Paris—I find myself in a new dilemma—We go to Fontenay-aux-Roses—My husband's duplicity—We are taken into the convent of the Sisters of Charity—Our experiences there—We leave the convent.

HAD I been free from anxiety on the subject of our future means of existence, our time in Paris, at this period, would have passed pleasantly enough. We were surrounded and *fêted* by excellent friends, who desired only to be useful to us, and to aid me in obtaining either my property or an allowance. I had, as already stated, lost all hope of assistance from the Marquis de Moustier, and had learnt, to my cost, that the Ottoman Embassy was the stronghold of my enemies. To remain inactive, a burden upon the ladies who had acted so generously towards us, was impossible, yet no sign was made from Constantinople.

No better fate befell a pressing appeal on our behalf, written and forwarded to Kibrizli Pasha by the Abbé Boré, who laid our position quite bare, and with a view to act upon my husband's pride, submitted to him that it was a dishonour, and a disgrace to his name and rank, to allow his wife and his children to be without means of existence, and dependents upon the benevolence of a few ladies. But it seemed as though hatred and a fierce desire for vengeance were, at that moment, the sentiments predominant in Kibrizli's mind, or his pride would assuredly have been moved.

The next attempt to influence him was made by the Countess de Bac, the Princess Davidoff, and other ladies whom they induced to unite with them in a petition which ought to have produced a favourable result, if the avenues to his better feelings had not been hermetically sealed against us. It is true a reply came, but only at the expiration of a month. It raised our hopes, doomed us to the most tantalizing suspense, and finally inflicted upon us the bitterest disappointment.

It is known that the great Paris Exhibition of the Industry of all Nations, opened in the month of May, 1867; and that amongst the magnates of the world who came to see it was His Sublime Highness the Sultan.

About the time the rumours of his intended visit began to acquire a certain degree of authority, and the period of it to be fixed—that is to say, nearly a month after the dispatch of the ladies' petition in our favour—the reply I have referred to reached the Abbé Boré through Monsieur Glavani, my banker at Constantinople. It was a simple request to be informed what amount per month would suffice for our maintenance. After the vicissitudes to which we had been so long exposed, and the privations we had undergone, our hearts leaped for very joy at the prospect of being at last adequately provided for. Our lady friends congratulated us upon the altered aspect of our affairs, and we sincerely thanked them for their interposition in our behalf, and complimented them upon their happy idea of the petition, to which alone we attributed the Pasha's apparently softened mood. Our answer became, for the moment, as grave a matter for consideration as an affair of state. In my time I had adjusted many, far more serious, with considerably less deliberation. The terms of it were settled at last, and having been duly signed and sealed, the missive was forwarded through the same channel as the communication had come, of which it was the acknowledgment.

Whilst we were in the most hopeful stage of expectancy, our friends the ladies left Paris for Boulogne-sur-Mer, and the term for which they had so kindly guaranteed us immunity from the cost of board and lodging expired. The end of June was close at hand, and although I had no reason to feel disappointed, no reply had yet arrived from my husband. I did not entertain the slightest suspicion of any disloyalty on his part in this matter; but, notwithstanding my daily increasing uneasiness at the delay, I strove to subdue my feverish impatience, still and ever hoping the next day or the next, would bring me the long-expected answer.

At this particular juncture we learnt that His Highness the Sultan would certainly arrive in Paris in the early days of July, accompanied by his Foreign Minister, Fuad Pasha, and by Rassim Pasha.

These two personages were amongst my husband's fiercest political enemies. By taking advantage of this circumstance, the way would be at once opened for me to obtain access to the Sultan, to lay my whole case before him, and to claim his interference and protection. I knew Fuad Pasha and his colleague would only be too pleased to expose their rival to the displeasure of their Sovereign, for the result would doubtless be Kibrizli's disgrace and ruin. In my desperate position, this was, perhaps, the most decisive step to take, to bring my affairs to a crisis. On the other hand, my husband had shown signs of relenting. He was even then—as I had reason to believe—making arrangements for the settlement upon me of an allowance sufficient to enable me and the children to live in a style in keeping with our rank. I desired too, for their sake, not to give him any cause to change his present favourable disposition towards us, but rather to encourage its developement. If he fulfilled the intention foreshadowed by his recent inquiry, I should speedily possess sufficient for all my requirements, and although by appealing to the Sultan I might obtain justice to the full extent of my rights, it would be at the expense of a man with whom I had spent the happiest days of my life, and whom—notwithstanding his cruel persecution of me and those dear to both of us—I still tenderly loved.

I found myself, under these circumstances, in a most awkward, indeed, a terrible dilemma. It was absolutely necessary to come to a decision. Ruin my husband, even injure him, I felt I could not. The only alternative was to wait for his answer to my latest appeal as patiently as possible.

But, if I remained in Paris until the Sultan arrived, I could not hope to escape from Fuad Pasha, who would assuredly hunt me up; and although he might not be able to alter my resolution to be no party to a hostile intrigue against my husband, although my own wrongs and the desire of redress would justify me in such a course, I felt I must inevitably become exposed to the most embarrassing importunities, and to the risk of being entrapped to commit some act I might afterwards regret.

Whilst I was revolving in my mind the modes I might adopt to avoid the embarrassments I foresaw and dreaded, and contemplating the chances which remained to me of obtaining justice, a new incident prompted me to a sudden decision.

The approaching visit of the Sultan inspired with hope of Imperial largess the thousand and one hangers-on upon Providence who are ever on the look out for substantial support for the establishments of which they are the patrons. Madame Davidoff was a very active and successful mendicant on behalf of her special *protégés*, and the Abbé Boré was equally zealous to obtain aid for the many benevolent schemes he was desirous to promote. Did they apprehend that were I to approach the Sultan, the extension of his bounty to me would diminish the amount he might have set aside for purposes of general benevolence, and their appeals be less generously responded to? I will not assert this; but I have never been able to comprehend why, at this particular juncture, both appeared animated with an anxious desire that I should leave Paris, or retire into a convent during the period of the Sultan's stay. The motive urged, was our personal safety. We were told that the Sultan might ask the Emperor to hand us over to our legal guardians in Constantinople, and that through the secret police this could easily be accomplished and nobody be the wiser. At first sight the danger appeared palpable, though a little reflection would have sufficed to satisfy me it was in a great measure imaginary. Disturbed as my mind was by conflicting thoughts, it is not surprising my fears should have taken the alarm. Retirement into a convent was not a pleasant prospect, but a brief stay in the country had a great charm. I yielded therefore to the suggestions of the friends I have named, and hearing of a cottage to be let at Fontenay-aux-Roses, I hired it, and hastened to occupy it.

We remained two months in this rustic retreat; two months of intense anxiety and wearying suspense. My funds being also in a very low state, we were often reduced to great straits, and compelled to submit to many privations.

During this anxious period, I had ample time to

repent of my misplaced confidence in my husband. So long as the Sultan was in Paris, even in England, I found excuses for Kibrizli's silence; but as week after week passed away, the suspicions I had sought to suppress asserted themselves with such irresistible force, I was compelled to yield to the conviction that I had been most grossly and cruelly duped.

Now, when it was too late I saw through the crafty design of my husband·in replying to the ladies' petition, and I despised, hated myself for allowing so transparent a trick to delude me. Until he knew that the Sultan would certainly go to Paris—and his position afforded him facilities for obtaining precise and early information of this—he had treated our appeals with cruel contempt; but no sooner did he acquire certain intelligence of his Sovereign's visit to the French capital, than prudence prompted the necessity of some step, which, whilst it should quiet me, left him free to act as he pleased towards us, and furnished him with a ready and a plausible defence in the event of an appeal to the Sultan during His Highness's sojourn in Paris.

His reply to the ladies' petition accomplished these several objects. It cajoled me by inspiring me with hope. If I waited patiently, the period of his Sovereign's stay in the French metropolis would be tided over, and the danger resulting from a disclosure averted. He could then resume his former policy of contemptuous silence to all our entreaties. In the event of an appeal to the Sultan, the reply to the ladies' petition could be produced as evidence of kind intentions towards us, and we should be practically left without justification for our resort, under these circumstances, to our Sovereign's sense of justice. All this I could see now; but it was too late—too late.

What to do I knew not. Day after day no reply came. One day I obtained confidential information that communications with the Ottoman Ambassador would produce no result, his secret instructions being to "let the women starve; only get them back." So my reiterated applications to that sublime official merely passed into his wastepaper basket, after an abstract of them had been made for my husband's delectation.

" Let the women starve; only get them back."

My husband knew, then, that we were, at that time, literally starving. What he did not know, nor believe, was that we were not to be got back; that his daughter, my poor Ayesha, preferred death, even from starvation, to living in luxury at Constantinople. Perhaps some suspicion of this at length occurred to him, and caused him to alter his tactics. In what respect, and through whose agency, it would be premature to disclose. We could not be bought nor starved into submission, but perhaps we might be betrayed into his power. At least the attempt could be made. Let the reader bear this intimation in mind.

We were now, after two months' residence at Fontenay-aux-Roses, reduced to such straits, that I solicited the kind interference of the Abbé Boré on our behalf, to obtain a small allowance for us from the Lazarists—the wealthy establishment to which he belonged—until something should be settled. This he was unable to accomplish, but he offered to procure admission for us, as boarders, into the Convent of the Ladies of Charity, at Arcueil, a kind of asylum for ladies of small means, or for such as destitution had thrown upon the bounty of their friends. For some time Ayesha resisted, having in as much horror the seclusion of the convent as of that of the harem. At length her disinclination yielded to necessity, and we were one evening conducted to the convent by the Princess Davidoff accompanied by an English lady.

Our new quarters were neither commodious nor

comfortable, and the truth may be told without prejudice. They consisted of one tolerable room of moderate dimensions, and of a kind of cell adjoining it, in which stood a small bedstead and one single chair. I appropriated this cell to my own use, for I could not have endured to subject my daughter to the discomforts of such a sleeping-place. Her bedroom was rather more conveniently fitted up, but—in harmony with the severe character of the establishment—the furniture did not consist of more than was barely necessary. We, nevertheless, accepted the refuge with heartfelt gratitude, though I must add, that the first night, before we retired, we sat awhile and shed not a few tears as our thoughts reverted to past days of magnificence and luxury, when we extended charity and never dreamt of being compelled to receive it.

Somewhat early next morning I was awakened by the sound of a gentle and strange footstep, and looking up, beheld a lady in the conventual dress, standing at the foot of my bed, knitting industriously. It was the Lady Superior, who came to inquire whether I needed anything. She was very condescending at first, but upon learning the circumstances under which the Abbé Boré had constituted us inmates of the establishment, that we were dependents upon its bounty, and not paying residents, her tone and manner suddenly changed, and we ceased to be objects worthy of any special attention.

In narrating our experiences in the convent, it must be understood that I record, with regret, any incidents which were disagreeable, and only because it is essential to the continuity of this history, that I should do so. I am grateful for all benefits received, but I feel that sentiments of gratitude ought not to cause me to conceal circumstances which influenced my course of action, notwithstanding that the revelation may not, in all cases, be flattering to individuals.

It is the result of my experience, that the vow of poverty and the renunciation of wealth, which is one of the essential conditions of conventual life, degenerate into avarice of the most exaggerated type, having for its sole aim and purpose the enriching of a particular establishment or order. The object being considered pre-eminently righteous, the means to the end are held to be sanctified. In the present instance, the Lady Superior was mortified to find we were likely to become burdens upon her establishment, and to impoverish its resources by just so much as the cost of our board and lodging would lay them under contribution. Her annoyance arose from no desire to derive any personal benefit from the sum at which our maintenance might be taxed, but from disappointment at the absence of all prospect of our contributing **ever so** small a share to the profits of the institution under her control. From the moment she made this discovery, her dominant idea was to get rid of us; **and to this end** she brought into operation all those petty means of vexation her position afforded her the opportunity of exercising: of which more in due course.

Our life was extremely monotonous, as might be expected, and our diet of the very plainest. *Café au lait* and dry bread in **the** morning. **At** noon, soup—as a rule very meagre indeed—a dish of meat and one of vegetables, with half a pint of extraordinary wine. The supper could be eaten without the remotest risk of nightmare. At first, the rations were absolutely insufficient, but my remonstrances led **to** an augmentation. The meagre days and fasts were over numerous, and honestly kept. On these occasions the flesh was unquestionably mortified, the corresponding benefit I consider doubtful. The religious exercises, in only the most essential of which **we** were expected to join, came in perpetual succession, and suggested rather forcibly the possibility of an excess of a good thing having its disadvantages. I know I shall be condemned as irreverent for saying so, but I am recording my true impressions. Such was, in its main features, the routine of our life in the Convent at Arcueil, during a period of three months. In this interval the Lady Superior was persistent in her endeavours to render it as uncomfortable as possible. All kinds of complaints of us were forwarded to the Abbé Boré. We were remiss in our attendances at religious celebrations. We roamed too much about in the gardens; we went out too often, we returned too late, we were, in fact, culpable on every point of the regulations of the establishment. The sisters, however, were very kind to us, and one or the other came every day to teach Ayesha French. The Abbé Boré was likewise a frequent visitor, and on these occasions took his share in her instruction. Under their combined guidance she advanced rapidly in her studies, but unhappily this kind of life did not harmonise with her mercurial temperament and habits, and even before the expiration of three months it had become unbearable.

I was not surprised this should be the case. She who had long pined for liberty, and had endured much in her attempt to secure it, had finally achieved it. She had fully enjoyed it for many months, and, to her, to whom everything was novel, exciting, interesting; whose notions of freedom were largely identified with indulgence in the pleasures and gaieties of polite society, the monotonous existence to which she now found herself, as it were, condemned, vividly revived recollections of the old days of imprisonment and restraint, and with the memory of these, the old desire to be free returned.

I strove my utmost to impress upon her the importance of our avoiding any rash step, such as quitting the convent, to excite the dissatisfaction of those who had so generously befriended us hitherto; and I represented that although we were literally eating the bread of charity, this was preferable to the prospect which, without funds or resources of any kind, must be in store for us, of enduring the pangs of hunger and the many privations attendant upon abject misery. We must, under any circumstances, await events, and it was better to do so where we were than incur new obligations.

But Ayesha was absolutely obdurate to every appeal. She fretted and chafed like a wild linnet in a cage. Her attention could not be confined to any single subject. The sisters continued to attend for the purpose of teaching her, but her mind wandered during her lessons. These devoted, patient, painstaking women, who pitied her as being a spoiled child, persevered with her to the last, though their looks denoted despair in their hearts. At last her excitement reached such a point, I seriously feared she would carry out a threat she had recently often made, that if a change were not made, she would run away and cast herself upon the protection of the first-comer.

Unfortunately the Abbé Boré was absent at this time, taking his vacation, or we might have received the advice of which we stood so greatly in need, or even his practical assistance. I therefore determined to see Madame Davidoff and tell her my new troubles. She expressed her regret that she could not help me in the way I wished, but she offered to receive us into her house. This proposition I felt constrained to decline, for I shrank from imposing ourselves as a burden upon her. I returned to the convent with a sad heart, and more embarrassed than ever, but was happily successful in inducing Ayesha to believe that the Abbé Boré would be back in a few days, when we should certainly receive his assistance in obtaining the means of changing our position. I also held out hope from another quarter.

There is a trite saying that when things come to

the worst they must perforce mend. This may be true, but often "the worst" lasts an over long time, and before the "mend" comes, the sufferer is driven to desperation. That our affairs appeared to have arrived at the worst, at this juncture, admitted of no doubt in my mind. I cannot say I expected the "mend" soon, for hope had well-nigh died out of my heart. Nevertheless, the change came far sooner than I could have anticipated; and singular to add, it originated in this very visit of mine to Princess Davidoff.

I met there a Polish gentleman, a major in a Turkish regiment, who had known me at Constantinople, whence he had recently come. He informed me that Zia Bey, ex-chamberlain to the Sultan, had expressed a great desire to see me. I therefore sent back a message that I would call upon him next morning. It was from this quarter I spoke of hope to Ayesha.

Zia Bey received me with great courtesy, and entered fully into the particulars of my position. He knew Kibrizli well; also the story of my divorce, and the ostensible reasons for it. He kindly gave me two hundred francs; concurred with me that it was desirable we should leave the convent, and promised to make me an allowance, until better times came.

He also told me that Mustapha Pasha—already referred to—had returned to Paris.

But why, it may be asked, did Zia Bey make this promise, and what was his real motive for befriending us? The simple fact is, we were just then pivots upon which turned certain ministerial intrigues at Constantinople.

I bear in mind that although I am not writing a political history, I am bound to furnish the reader with a clue to the events of which I was continually being made the victim, and without which the singular and sudden changes in my fortunes would appear inexplicable.

I must state, then, that a political party, calling itself "Young Turkey," had been formed in Constantinople, the object of which was to promote administrative and other reforms, including representative government, responsible ministries, and irresponsible sovereignty. To this party belonged Mustapha Pasha, Zia Bey, and the Polish major. Mustapha was immensely rich, therefore independent of everybody, unambitious of office, and fearless in the expression of his opinions. As a matter of course, Fuad Pasha and Ali Pasha were his political opponents, they being the chief Ministers of the reigning Sultan, Abdul Assiz. The war against the system of which they were the official agents, commenced by a visit made by Mustapha Pasha to the Sultan, to whom he exposed the flagitious abuses committed under the seals of office, the barefaced peculations, extortions, and impositions practised in every department, the utter absence of control over the administrators of any department of the State, and the certain result to the Empire. In making this revelation, however, for the guidance of the Sultan, he enjoined him to secrecy, which the Sultan promised. But scarcely had Mustapha quitted the royal presence, than His Imperial Highness sent for Fuad and Ali Pasha, and upbraided them furiously. They denied, of course, the allegations brought against them, and quitted their master, breathing vengeance against Mustapha, who, being timely warned of danger, hastily quitted Constantinople, and made for Paris, with his suite. He had been already some time there when I arrived.

Although Kibrizli was not associated with the "Young Turkey" party, the removal of Ali and Fuad Pasha from office would have once more raised him into power. He had, indeed, no sympathy with reformers of any kind, therefore no friendship for Mustapha and his friends; and they on their side, regarding him as incorrigibly addicted to the vicious system they desired to reform, had no extravagant liking for him. Their policy, therefore, was to worry and annoy him and the party to which he belonged, in every possible manner, and as my divorce and downfall were known to have been the price Kibrizli paid for his retention of office, I and Ayesha became instruments in their hands—though we knew it not at that time—through whom they could mortify Kibrizli; for to help his wife and children, whom he was leaving to starvation, would be a humiliation to him and a public scandal.

But although Mustapha Pasha left Constantinople, the party of which he was the head continued its intrigues, and his friends, Zia Bey, the Pole, Aga Effendi, Djamil Bey, Nouroid Bey, Reschid Bey, and other leaders, got up a formidable conspiracy, which included some 30,000 associates, its object being to overthrow the ministry by force at any cost, and even, if necessary, to dispose of the Sultan. The plot, however, did not come to a head. One of the conspirators betrayed it to the police, and thus prevented its explosion; but the parties to it I have named contrived to effect their escape and to rejoin Mustapha Pasha in Paris, where they became dependents upon his bounty. When the Sultan came to Paris, Mustapha contrived to regain his sovereign's favour, and shortly after repaired to Constantinople, upon a rumour that Ali Pasha and Fuad Pasha had been deposed. Upon his arrival there, he found these ministers still in power, and thereupon returned to Paris. It was the news of this return which Zia Bey communicated to me.

The reader will now understand that Zia Bey received an allowance from Mustapha Pasha, that out of it he made me one, and that he did this to annoy Kibrizli. Whether Mustapha knew of Zia's liberality, I am not able to assert, but subsequent events impressed me with the belief that he did.

The prospect of even a temporary allowance, filled me with joy. At least I should have the means of existence, pending the result of further attempts to force my husband to do us justice, and I was better pleased on my daughter's account than on my own, that this unexpected assistance had come; for my sole happiness centred in hers, and the gratification of her wishes was my great desire. She ran short of clothes, so my first impulse led me to the Temple, the Israelite mart for cheap, though not new, apparel; and I laid out perhaps an undue proportion of my tiny fortune in changes of suits most becoming to her; then hurried back in a hackney-coach to the convent to lay them at her feet.

I know this piece of extravagance will be condemned as an unpardonable imprudence, as the very height of improvidence; but a mother's love is unsusceptible of selfish considerations, and the delight of ministering to a beloved child's gratification outweighs all other sentiments. Many a mere momentary happiness is dearly purchased; but what happiness greater or more legitimate than that of witnessing the delight of a child on receiving a parent's gift unexpectedly, and those, the very objects upon which its young heart is set? Such felicity is worth a sacrifice, for none brings purer joy. I appeal to mothers if this is not so.

Ayesha, a woman in years, in many respects one in experience, was nevertheless a complete child in her impulses and in her ignorance of the world and its ways. An infant of five years old could not have given way to more extravagant demonstrations of wild delight, on receiving a new doll, than did Ayesha on seeing her new clothes. She shrieked, she laughed, she cried, she leaped, and danced about, and embraced me over and over again. Nothing would content her but to deck herself out in her newly-purchased habiliments, and show herself in them to the sisters and the other inmates of the convent. It was a happy day for her; for me, one to be remembered.

I placed the balance of my two hundred francs, namely, eighty, in the hands of the Lady Superior, informing her it was for safe keeping, and that we should leave the convent as soon as I had found an apartment to suit us. I lost no time in seeking one, and having succeeded at last in finding what I required in the Rue d'Isly, prepared to bid adieu to the establishment at Arcueil.

On claiming my small stock of money of the Lady Superior, I was astounded to meet with a refusal to return it. I had been three months in the house, with my daughter, living upon its funds, we had not contributed in any way towards them, and she had understood that the sum placed in her hands was an instalment towards the cost of our maintenance. I pointed out to her that such an assumption was unfounded, that I had been placed there by the Abbé Boré, of whose arrangements I was wholly ignorant, and that if anything were due for my maintenance, she must look to the Abbé for it: but I wanted the small sum in her hands, and should insist upon its being returned to me. Thus pressed, the Lady Superior handed me back my money, and I subsequently learnt that the Abbé Boré had to pay the sum his " dear Sister in God" claimed for our board and lodging.

Under these circumstances we quitted the convent, after an affectionate leave-taking of the kind, good sisters.

CHAPTER VIII.

Fresh disappointments—Saÿd Acha, the bankrupt merchant—A new acquaintance—Ayesha receives an offer of marriage—We take a journey into Brittany—Our host—Mysterious incidents—Ayesha accepts the proposal for her hand.

For the space of two months we seemed to be in paradise. Ayesha soon threw off the morbid depression induced by confinement, and surrendered herself entirely to the luxury of unrestraint. That the mere consciousness of not being confined within the four dead walls of a convent; of not being restricted to eat, drink, sleep, rise, and pray by the clock, should be to her a supreme pleasure, may appear a paradox to many, yet not wholly so to those who will take the pains to consider what her life had been. Her wild, impulsive, restless nature, so much like what mine was at her age, rebelled against restraint of any kind; and her long sojourn within the precincts of the harem, had been one protracted, continuous contradiction of her intense longing for perfect freedom over her own actions.

To feel, to know, she was now not subject to any control, was therefore to her of itself a positive enjoyment, and in it she revelled to her heart's content. We were both happy, for we thought we had at last found a friend.

Our happiness proved only of brief duration. On our leaving the convent, Zia Bey gave me five hundred francs, which I husbanded scrupulously. One morning, at the expiration of about two months, the Major brought me a note from him, announcing his departure for England. It also contained another advance of funds, but it conveyed the intimation of Zia's regret that he should be obliged to discontinue affording me assistance, as Mustapha Pasha had ceased making him an allowance; hence his own departure for London.

Accustomed though I was to vicissitudes of various kinds, I was not yet hardened to regard without emotion a new prospect of penury and privation. Zia Bey's communication was a most painful surprise, but I could not expect help from him under the circumstances he had urged as his excuse for its discontinuance. Not until much later did I learn that the differences between Mustapha and my husband had been made up, and that the cessation of assistance to me was the condition of its continuance from Mustapha to Zia.

We were now once more left to the mercy of fate. Our sole hope, to which we clung with the tenacity of desperation, lay in the effort the Abbé Boré was still making, through friends at Constantinople, to obtain our rights. Our only resource was to husband the last gift of Zia Bey, and wait, as patiently as we might, the issue of the Abbé's negociations.

But Fortune's wheel suddenly took another, and, as it turned out, a most singular turn.

A note reached me one morning, bearing the signature "Saÿd Acha." He was a merchant, who, having failed in business at Constantinople—some twenty years ago at that time—had decamped and come to Paris. He had heard of us, and wrote, soliciting leave to call upon us. Thinking he might be useful, I acceded to his request, and he came. He was about sixty years of age now, could not speak a word of French, and was still poor. He expressed a deep interest in us, and approved of our plan of awaiting the result of our friend's application on our behalf for the redress so obstinately denied to us.

I did not know that this man was, at that very

time, a spy in the secret service of the Turkish Embassy.

After a few visits, he spoke of a friend of his, whom he was in the habit of meeting at a café, and whom he should, with my permission, be greatly pleased to introduce. This gentleman, he said, was extremely partial to Orientals, and passed much time in the company of those who were to be met with in Paris. He was not only wealthy, but belonged to one of the best families in Brittany, and was altogether a most eligible acquaintance. Thus recommended, I gave Saÿd Acha permission to present his friend.

Our new visitor was a man of about thirty-three years of age, tall, well made, having an agreeable countenance, and polished manners. He produced upon me not quite a favourable impression, and one tinged with a degree of suspicion. He was soft-spoken and meek, seldom raising his voice above a loud and well-modulated whisper, and he rolled his eyes nervously, which made him look askance at the person he was speaking to. He seemed highly delighted to make our acquaintance, paid us many compliments, and obtained permission to renew his visits.

These soon became very frequent, and I could

not conceal from myself that he seemed amazingly smitten with my daughter. He professed to be greatly captivated by Ayesha's ingenuousness, and gradually hinted that the desire of his life had been to marry an Oriental lady—one wholly uninitiated in the duplicities of Western society and fashionable life—whom he could train and educate, and, in fact, fashion to his mind, and for himself alone. He did not seek a dowry. He was possessed of wealth, owned a château in the Morbihan, and several farms, and had no incumbrances; and a young woman, who would return devotion to him for his devotion to her, might be supremely happy.

These indirect appeals became so frequently the subject of his conversation, that I thought it high time to sound Ayesha upon the question of a second marriage. To enable her to contract a new alliance, the Pope's dispensation would be necessary, notwithstanding that she had been legally divorced from her husband, Ferideh's son, Shevket, according to Mussulman forms. The dispensation could probably be easily obtained, through the Abbé Boré and M. de Monroi, and this obstacle removed, there seemed no valid reason why, if an offer were made to her, she should refuse it. But Ayesha declined, saying she did not like Monsieur Questel

—this was our Breton friend's name,—she doubted him, and fancied him insincere; against which stout reasons I could urge no argument.

Day by day, however, this situation became more delicate. Neither Ayesha nor I could any longer ignore the tendency of M. Questel's hints—although he had not formally proposed—nor the direct purpose of his attentions. I seriously contemplated the bringing of his visits to a close, and was casting about for a fair excuse, when my embarrassment was relieved by M. Questel himself, who offered Ayesha his hand "and his whole heart," as he said, and we should have our own time to consider his proposal.

Our critical position, the vivid recollection of our sufferings, the uncertainty of the issue of our friends' negociations at Constantinople, these combined to warp my judgment, and to influence me to lay aside my first impressions of Questel, whose offer would, if accepted, place us for ever beyond the reach of want, and secure us peace and quietness. But Ayesha still refused. At length, yielding to my representations, she consented to accept him, for the sake of a quiet life, provided it could be ascertained that M. Questel's means were such as he had represented. I communicated her reply to

M. Questel; and so far from objecting to a proposition of my own that we should ourselves go down into Brittany and inspect his estates and farms and château, he promoted the plan with noticeable alacrity, and approved of it as highly reasonable and business-like. With this understanding he left us, for the purpose of preparing for our réception, saying this was necessary, for his people were, like all the Bretons, stupid, though honest, and very rough. He promised to write to us without delay.

M. Questel's ready acquiescence in my proposition, sufficed to dispel any doubts I had entertained of his sincerity, and I could see it had also produced the same effect upon Ayesha. We were both of us pleased and encouraged, whilst the prospect of happiness for her was at least as good as any young girl in Turkey could hope for. The match was not, in principle, different—with respect to the girl's inclinations—from the majority of marriages in France, which are rather contracts for convenience' sake, or for mutual interest, than unions based upon reciprocal affection. In the present instance it was even, to all appearance, unselfish on the side of the suitor, for he brought the fortune, and sought neither dowry nor prospective advantages, and he had to incur the chances of a reciprocity of affection. It was true Ayesha might come to love him, in course of time, though at present indifferent; and after all, no violence was offered to her feelings. Full leisure for consideration was afforded us, and she remained free to withdraw from the engagement at any moment.

In order not to lose the earliest intelligence of any communication from Constantinople, we informed the Abbé Boré we had been invited to spend a time at a country-seat, and gave him an address to which he could write; but we kept quite silent with regard to everybody else, for I felt apprehensive of any accident which might interfere with the success of the present project.

M. Questel kept his promise. Within a few days he sent us money for our journey and also railway rugs; for the weather was now cold. We started from the Mont-Parnasse station at half-past seven in the morning, taking the express train to Vannes, according to our instructions. Our journey occupied twelve hours, and we were glad enough when it came to an end, for we were most terribly jolted and fatigued.

M. Questel was at the station waiting to receive us. Probably out of compliment to us, he wore a fez, the modern Turkish coïf. I noticed he was dressed with remarkable elegance. A carriage was in attendance, to which he conducted us with a deference not to be exceeded had we been princesses; and to me he paid most special attention. It was a lovely, clear, moonlight night, but we could not discern much of the country. It was nine o'clock before we reaced the château at Kerbeque, near a place called Noyalo.

Immediately on our arrival, M. Questel delivered us over into the hands of a waiting-maid, who conducted us to the apartments prepared for us; a bed-room with two beds in it, and a sitting-room, extremely well furnished, and even fitted up with elegance and numerous small comforts.

The maid presently preceded us down-stairs into the dining-room, which we found brilliantly illuminated, and the dinner just served up. Besides our special maid, who remained in the room to assist, there were two others and a man-servant.

The repast was of the choicest kind, indicating luxurious tastes on the part of our host. I ventured upon a polite remonstrance that he should have deemed it worth while to treat us so sumptuously; but he protested, as emphatically as so very meek speaking an individual could protest, that he had really gone to no excess, it was his customary fare, his "ordinaire"; he would, on the contrary, have been only too glad to show us a little extra attention, but really, in that Bretagne of theirs, there was no possibility of getting any dish decently prepared, and to keep a chef-de-cuisine for his own self, living as he did a solitary life, was of course out of the question; but all that would be altered in due time.

The attentions of our host during the dinner were most minute and delicate, without being obtrusive. He assisted us to the choicest tit-bits; apologized for not being able to offer us a selection of more than four kinds of wine, and for the failure of the dessert. I need scarcely observe that the dessert was various, select, and abundant, and that excellent "vin-ordinaire," choice Margaux, delicate Burgundy, and Cliquot, presented a wine-list more than sufficient for two ladies unaccustomed to fermented liquors of any kind. Nor were those liqueurs wanting which the gentler sex are reported to prefer. In fact, absolutely nothing was needed at this Sybarite feast, notwithstanding the protestations of M. Questel to the contrary.

I must make the humiliating confession that I vastly enjoyed this banquet, and that my spirits rose with the occasion. M. Questel made himself highly agreeable, by keeping up a lively conversation, which ran upon the topics of the day and the small scandals current in the fashionable world, interspersed with amusing anecdotes, and now and then an original observation. He endeavoured, but in vain, to draw out Ayesha. She was dull, silent, and unamiable, and our host must have been blind not to perceive that his civilities did not please her. The truth is, that not liking the host, she did not care to play the hypocrite by responding to his courtesies.

It was late before we retired for the night. M. Questel, following the waiting-maid, preceded us to the door of our apartment, where he quitted us, with many a salutation, saying he should watch over us; a mild joke, as I presently discovered when he explained that his own sleeping-room was on the fourth floor; having discharged which he bade us good night.

We were allowed to sleep without being disturbed, until we descended, of our own accord, once more into the dining-room. Our host was already in attendance, and on a scarcely perceptible sign from him, the early or first breakfast was brought in by our waiting-maid. The coffee and cream were delicious, the bread and butter equally so. After the meal, we were invited to inspect the house, and accordingly we followed M. Questel over it.

The château, prettily situated in a park near one end of a plain, appeared to be of recent date, as I subsequently learnt was the fact, having been constructed by the present owner, after a design of his own. It was a round tower, four stories high, with garrets in the roof, and built of white stone. The master's suite of apartments occupied the fourth floor, commanding from each window an extensive prospect. In all, the tower contained ten rooms. The drawing-room, or salon, covered one floor, and was lofty and spacious. The view from every window was exceedingly pleasant: on one side a stretch of sea; on another the undulating open country; on another an extensive plain, through which meandered a small river; on a fourth a garden, shrubbery, and other grounds, with fields beyond and meadows, and clumps and avenues of tall trees. All the rooms were well furnished, and in the drawing-room I observed two pianofortes.

After our examination of the interior, our host conducted us to visit the outer premises. The servants' offices and the stables were detached from the house. In the coach-house stood three carriages.

Every place was thrown open to us. We passed through the garden and the adjoining grounds, and came to a neat pavilion, at the end of a secluded walk, and within a few dozen yards of the sea at low tide. A flight of stone steps led from the pavilion into the water, and at the foot of these a boat was moored. This was the bathing pavilion. All this was charming, and I observed that Ayesha appeared interested in what might become her new domain.

We returned to the château, by which time the second breakfast, the "déjeûner à la fourchette," was ready. It matched the dinner of the previous evening, and M. Questel's attentions did not flag. After breakfast, he proposed a drive. One of the carriages was accordingly ordered up, and we were driven over his estate, and round about it, he pointing out his farms and lands, and dwelling upon the absence of any present inducement on his part to render them more remunerative to him as a landlord, though, were he married, he should necessarily seek to increase his income by raising the farmers' rents. We were told that all his property lay within so convenient a distance in the neighbourhood of the château, that he did not require the services of a land-steward, but collected his rents himself, at the château, at stated periods of the year, and also attended to and directed such improvements as he found desirable, either for the convenience of his tenants or to suit his own wishes.

Dinner-time came, and the repast resembled in delicacy and choice the one of the day before; similar select dishes, the same profusion of wines, the same abundant dessert, and the same scrupulous attentions on the part of the host.

We remained one month the guests of M. Questel, during which period our repasts, now served at hours fixed for our convenience, were of the same luxurious character. His courtesy never flagged. Never, at the height of my prosperity, when adored by my husband and holding his seals, and when I exercised a sovereign authority, did my attendants show me more deference, or seek to forestall my wishes more anxiously than did M. Questel. Did I recline on the couch? he was at my side to place a pillow under my head; Did I lounge in an easy-chair? he was at my feet with a foot-stool. Were we going out? he took the most minute precautions to preserve me from draughts, and every night he performed an exemplary pilgrimage to the door of our apartment, always bidding us good-night in the same scrupulously polite manner.

All this was exceedingly pleasant, and appearances were thus far satisfactory. I had, however, been struck with one singular fact. M. Questel, ever ready, ever apparently delighted, to take a turn with us, either in the carriage or for a walk, never allowed me to go out alone. I made several attempts, but strange to say he was at my side ere I had advanced many steps beyond the threshold. I could not comprehend how he possibly contrived to know my intentions, for I could not suspect him of watching me, yet he always seemed to meet or to overtake me by the merest accident. This odd circumstance much puzzled me, and not only stimulated my curiosity but made me determine I would take the earliest opportunity of evading his vigilance. It came within a few days of our departure, and quite unexpectedly.

Ayesha had, on one particular day, manifested a great desire to see the country in a different direction from any in which we had yet been driven. M. Questel, of course, made it a point of complying with her wish, and asked me to prepare to accompany them. Under the pretext of slight indisposition I declined to go out, although I perceived he was somewhat disappointed at my refusal, and suggested Ayesha's deferring her ride until another day. But she did not care to renounce her trip, and he was compelled to leave me behind. Here, then, at last, was my opportunity.

As soon as I felt satisfied they were far enough on their way to render it safe for me to venture out, I started on my voyage of discovery, my object being to make inquiry of the neighbours, if I could come across any, as to the position and character of our honey-mouthed host. After wandering about some time, in my endeavours to find a road out of the grounds leading to somewhere, and which did not bring me up against a stone wall, or a ditch, or a hedge, I got into the highway and had not proceeded far before I came to a sort of wine-shop and "restaurant," standing in isolation by the roadside. A decent looking woman stood bare-armed behind her counter, either waiting upon Providence or for customers; and the latter seemed to be few and far between. Being tired, after my anxious peregrinations, I asked for refreshment, and soon got into conversation with her.

Yes! She knew Monsieur Questel. They—she and her husband—were tenants of his, and held the house and a small piece of land attached to it. Certainly, he had other property. The château was his? Yes, and he had several farms. An excellent landlord, a most kind good man. Rich? Oh, considerably! A great pity he was not married. It would be such a good thing for the poor if he came to live upon his estate.

Such was the result of my first inquiry. I bade my informant good day, and a turn of the road, some distance farther on, brought me to a farm, which I recognized as one of those M. Questel had pointed out as his. A lack of hospitality to the extent of a chair to a fatigued wayfarer is not a failing of the Bretons; and whilst resting again here, I elicited from the stranger, information concerning M. Questel, confirmatory of the good account I had already received of him. This decided me. I returned home satisfied he had not misrepresented his means. Nevertheless, there occurred two other circumstances, in the course of this month's visit, which also singularly puzzled me.

Regarding myself as the probable directress of M. Questel's establishment, and having received from him *carte blanche* to roam all over the premises, I did not scruple to visit his own suite of rooms. One of these was a kind of lumber-room, but it was fitted up with shelves and large pigeon-holes. If M. Questel, instead of being a wealthy landed proprietor, had been a dealer in ancient apparel, laying in stock to set up a frippery, I should not have felt surprised on finding in such a place as this, a lumber-room with so many bundles of old clothes. They lay on the shelves in heaps, they were tucked away into the pigeon-holes, they were stowed into corners, and were lying about anywhere and everywhere. Blouses, coats, and unmentionables of all colours, cuts, and dimensions, and in various stages of advanced wear, met the prying eye; hats and caps, waistcoats, boots, shoes, and slippers; old linen, sadly in need of fumigation; pieces of cloth and ancient rags, completed the nomenclature of the effects contained in this Blue Beard's cupboard. What could this odd fancy for a museum of worn-out apparel possibly indicate? Could M. Questel—always so scrupulously neat and elegant in his own dress that one might have believed he kept himself snugly shut up in a band-box when not on view—be afflicted with an old-clothes' mania? Why—he so good and charitable—did he not give his cast-off raiment to the poor? Yet, another idea! Was there a periodical distribution of these effects, and did he lay his friends under contribution to swell the stock to be ceremoniously given away? The more I endeavoured to solve this mystery, the less satisfactory were my conclusions. I took an opportunity of asking M. Questel why he kept such a lot of rubbish. He merely smiled meekly, and replied, under his breath, that this was "one of his little secrets."

I found it out, for all that! With the connivance of Ayesha, I obtained two or three other opportunities of renewing my acquaintanceship with our neighbours, although I durst never venture beyond the immediate precincts of the château. I did not feel inclined openly to oppose what I perceived was a peculiarity in M. Questel—an indisposition to allow me to go out alone—and at the same time the sense of a restraint upon my actions was irksome. Necessity, therefore, compelled me to manœuvre a little for the gratification of my wish. With this view, I enlisted Ayesha into my service, without explaining I was secretly making inquiries concerning her suitor's position and character, but leaving her to understand that it was a whim of mine to take an occasional solitary walk, which I could not indulge in without offending M. Questel. So it happened that I one day fell in with an old woman, who sat spinning in her doorway, and whom, as an excuse for addressing her, I asked to direct me back to the château by the nearest path. The very mention of the château was an "open sesame" to conversation on the subject of its owner. I gleaned nothing from the old lady to his disadvantage but one fact, which threw a degree of light upon the old clothes mystery: he was very good and kind, "but oh, Madame, he is such a miser."

Questel, so lavish in his household expenditure, keeping twice as many servants as the maintenance of the establishment in order required: Questel a miser! What a contradiction! What inconsistency of character! But then human nature is made up of inconsistencies, and every one has his own peculiar failing. Thus I reasoned as I wended my way back, yet without being able to reconcile the new fact with my experience of the man.

The other circumstance was even still more mysterious, nor did I ever succeed in clearing it up, save by a conjecture, to be communicated later, when the reader will be able to arrive at his own conclusions upon the additional knowledge he will have acquired.

From a window in my bed-room, as from one in the drawing-room, I commanded a complete view of the garden-grounds. Early one morning, looking out from mine to ascertain the state of the weather, I observed a strange man in one of the pathways. He wore the dress of a provincial peasant, but something in his gait satisfied me he was in a disguise. With furtive steps he made his way into a remote corner, where he took up his station under a tree. He held something huddled up under his arm, beneath his blouse, or smock-frock, and looked up at the windows of the fourth floor, where, as already stated, Questel's apartments were. At first I thought of mentioning the circumstance to Ayesha, then of warning Questel, but a moment's reflection sufficed to convince me that either course would be imprudent. I could at least watch and await the issue. In the course of a few minutes, I saw Questel leave the house, and after glancing up at my window, proceed towards the spot where the strange man stood. The two seemed to exchange a few sentences, as if both were in somewhat of a hurry, and then the stranger withdrew from its hiding-place what he held concealed there, and handed it to Questel. It was a canvas bag containing money. This done, the men parted, Questel returning stealthily—as it appeared to me—to the house, his friend, or agent, or accomplice, departing by the path just mentioned.

What could this mysterious proceeding mean?

The incident produced so strange an impression upon me, that I was disturbed in mind the whole day. I said nothing about it to Ayesha, but resolved to watch narrowly for any farther developement of the mystery.

Three days after, a repetition of the same incident occurred, and so it went on afterwards, at intervals of two or three days during our stay. On one of these occasions, an altercation seemed to be going on, for I noticed much gesticulation on both sides, and it struck me as especially singular, that M. Questel, habitually so bland and mild, should suddenly be capable of an animated conversation. That same morning, at breakfast, he placed in my daughter's hands a bag containing—as he said—a trifle of five thousand francs in gold, which he begged her to accept to purchase jewellery with when she returned to Paris, as a reminder of her journey into Brittany. But Ayesha refused the gift and pushed the bag away again.

"Yet," thought I, "this man is reputed to be a miser."

As may be supposed, I exhausted my ingenuity in conjecturing solutions of the enigma of these strange meetings. We were near the sea, with every facility for contraband trade. Was Questel in league with a gang of smugglers? Or, was he the head of a band of coiners, or robbers? I dismissed these surmises in due course of time, and after making the inquiries already narrated; but the incident left an uncomfortable impression. Not till some length of time after did I make it known to Ayesha.

As the days passed away I began to feel constrained to speak to my daughter respecting her intentions, for, remain under this man's roof we could not, decorously, under the circumstances. I found that his unwearied attentions, his kindness, his uniform equable temper, his mildness of disposition as exhibited in his relations with his household, had produced a certain favourable impression upon her, and that although she did not feel any affection for him, she began to like him better: "He is so good, mamma!"

So, having agreed that the moment had arrived for a decision, and that the venture should be made, we intimated to our host our disinclination to tax his hospitality any longer. He protested, naturally enough, that we were welcome to remain as much longer as we chose, but if we had resolved to leave him, at least he might venture to hope he had not in any way failed in his duties as host, and perhaps he might farther venture to solicit the favour of a reply to the proposal he had had the temerity to make, and which had procured him the distinguished honour of our visit to his humble dwelling.

What reply but the one was to be made? The die was cast. Ayesha accepted him, and I embraced my new son-in-law, who most respectfully kissed my hand, then that of his affianced wife.

CHAPTER IX.

We go to London—My daughter's marriage—We return into Brittany—I am watched—I evade M. Questel's vigilance—My new relations—Extraordinary revelations.

M. QUESTEL had in the course of our various conversations informed me that his father was dead, and that his mother was an English lady, belonging to a family of great distinction, who, after her husband's decease, had returned to her native country, and was then living in London upon her income. It did not startle me, therefore, when he suggested that, on her account, the marriage should take place in that city, according to the forms of the Catholic Church. I could urge no reasonable objection to this proposition, for it was plausible enough, and the mother's presence on such an occasion seemed especially desirable. We agreed, therefore, to comply with his desire.

In the arrangements for our journey, and in every imaginable way, M. Questel was attentive to the last degree, and in the minor courtesies of daily life was even more scrupulously polite than ever. Indeed, his assiduities became almost painful to me. I had endeavoured to reason myself out of my first impressions of him, and had succeeded to the extent of believing they were erroneous; but there remained an under-current of vague mistrust which, in spite of my efforts to suppress it, would continually bring to the surface the stray straws to which my misgivings clung, giving to these a sudden and serious importance. His very excess of politeness, flattering at first, became wearisome, and at last was positively painful. There was in it something studied and deliberate; although if I had been challenged to lay my finger upon a single act of his—in his almost hourly intercourse with us—which gave evidence of insincerity, I should most assuredly have failed.

It was arranged we should repair to London without any unnecessary delay. In Paris we put up at an hotel in the Rue du Bac, Faubourg St. Germain, whence we started for London by way of Boulogne and Folkestone. On board the steamer an odd incident occurred, which again renewed my old suspicions, and gave me a most unfavourable idea of my intended son-in-law's veracity. I have stated that when he met us at the station at Vannes he appeared in the fez. This coif he continued to wear, and in Paris I observed that he had made an investment in a new one. It now attracted the notice of a gentleman, a fellow-passenger, and he presently engaged in conversation with Questel, who probably thought the rolling of the vessel had made me close my ears as well as my eyes. It was in reply to an observation made by this gentleman that Questel said he had just come from the East with his wife and his mother-in-law. We certainly were travelling West, and prospectively Ayesha and I stood towards him in the relation he had indicated, but the fact was as yet unaccomplished: he had imposed upon our fellow-passenger, and told him a downright falsehood. The motive, save to make himself for the moment interesting to his interlocutor, I could not divine.

I do not know where Questel lodged us in London, nor in what neighbourhood. It was in a grand, fine house, magnificently furnished, and where we were sumptuously provided for. We did not, however, remain there more than four or five days, and were removed into some large foreign hotel in Leicester Square. Monsieur Questel, still unremitting in his attentions, busied himself in making purchases for us of dresses and jewelry, and other articles, regardless of our protests against his extravagance, which he met by the most vehement assurances that nothing could be too good for us.

It had been settled that the marriage should take place by licence, but Monsieur Questel startled us by an announcement of his intention to have it solemnized according to the forms of the Protestant Church, giving as one reason his inveterate dislike to Roman Catholic priests. In reply to my objections—for I felt certain scruples on this score—he urged that one form of marriage was as good as another, and he had decided for the Protestant form, because it offered the immense advantage of rendering unnecessary a dispensation from the Pope, and, as a consequence, the avoidance of delay. This explanation satisfied me, and it was decided that the ceremony should take place at the Church of St. James', Piccadilly.

Several times during this interval Monsieur Questel referred to his mother in terms indicating extreme annoyance at her absence from London, but leaving us to understand that she would arrive for the ceremony. As it was winter-time, and the snow lay heavily on the ground, I expressed my sympathy with the lady's disinclination to move about in such weather, and not to come to London until the last moment. I thought it odd, however, that he did not introduce us to any of her grand connexions, nor to any of his own friends.

A few days before the one fixed for the marriage I received a letter which compelled me to start immediately for Paris. It related to Djehad, on whose behalf some interest had been exercised to secure him admission into the corps of the Pope's Zouaves. The intelligence was to the effect that the corps would leave for Rome on a particular day, and Djehad must present himself at headquarters at once or lose his nomination. This unexpected incident prevented my being present at the marriage, but it was agreed that my daughter and her husband should rejoin me as speedily after it as possible.

Under these circumstances the wedding was solemnized on the twenty-second of January, 1868; and M. Questel and his bride joined me in Paris shortly afterwards.

We remained in Paris only a very few days, and then returned to the château in Brittany. Here the old course of life was resumed, and the old manifestations of civility and minute attention to me were as marked and particular as of yore. With them, too, came the former restrictions upon my personal freedom. I could not stir out unattended by Questel: could not get away half a dozen yards from the door, but my vigilant son-in-law appeared at my elbow. Scarcely did he leave me an hour without looking after me upon some trivial pretext. This constant espionage produced a nervous, anxious state of mind, which entirely deprived me of rest, and set me considering what might be his reason for cutting me off from free intercourse with our neighbours, or I might even now say my neighbours. I resolved, however, to break through this insufferable restraint, and my first step was to endeavour to learn how he contrived to know when I quitted the house, though I did not make known my intention prior to making the attempt. An examination of the position of his apartments satisfied me that this post of observation commanded a full view of the door and of the paths of egress and ingress from and to the house, and that he must be constantly on the watch. I might, indeed, have discovered as much in the earlier days had his attentions not hoodwinked my judgment by quieting my suspicions. Once, however, convinced that I was really systematically watched from one of his windows, the conclusion was forced upon me that there must be some cogent reason for such a proceeding, and I determined to act upon my conviction that his jealousy covered another of his "little secrets."

Having well reconnoitred the ground, I concluded that by keeping close to the wall I might evade my spy's vigilant glance, and secure impunity by leaving the house early in the morning. The very next day I put my plan in execution, and accomplished my purpose.

Although during my former stay my opportunities of a solitary walk had been few, I had, in our later rides and promenades, closely observed localities, and having now fixed upon a strategic point of departure, I formed my plans for a complete campaign of inquiry. Proceeding, then, in quite a new direction, I walked on until I came to an old house situated in the middle of a garden. In the court-yard were three women, one in the garb of a person of the better class, and wearing a coif like a sister or a nun, the two others, servant-maids, in huge wooden shoes, their arms and the upper part of their massive shoulders bare. The three were busy preparing food for fowls and pigs.

I laid my hand upon the gate, and had time to take note of the group before the chief member of it perceived me. She looked sharply up as soon as she caught a glimpse of something moving, and left off her occupation. The others almost as soon did the same, staring at me as I advanced.

"Madame," said I, addressing the lady in the nun's cap, "may I take the liberty of asking to be allowed to rest myself for a few minutes?"

"But, certainly, Madame, with pleasure. Come in, Madame."

I was conducted into a sort of kitchen, and a wooden chair was set for my accommodation. The lady took another, and sat down opposite to me.

"Madame is—is from the château, I presume?" said she.

"I am, Madame. Do you know the owner?"

"Monsieur Questel? Oh, certainly."

"You have known him long?"

The lady smiled.

"I see," said I; "then you know him well."

"If I did not, Madame, I do not know who should. I am Madame Questel."

I repeated her two last words in a tone which indicated my astonishment.

"Yes, Madame," continued the lady, "I am his sister-in-law, his own brother's wife."

"Oh, indeed! I did not know he had any such near relatives. He never mentioned the fact to me. Indeed, he intimated that he had no family connexions living except his mother."

It was Madame Questel's turn to echo my last words.

"His mother! His mother living!"

"Yes! So he told me. She is a grand lady of high family, living in London on her income."

Madame Questel seemed struck dumb. Her pleasant countenance assumed an expression of blank astonishment, and the colour died out of her cheeks. At length she exclaimed, bringing her hands together with a clap and intertwining her fingers:

"*Grand Dieu!* He told you that? Why his mother, poor soul, has been dead some years!"

"It is, perhaps, a second wife," I suggested.

"But no, Madame! Jean-Marie's father did not marry again."

"Jean-Marie!" I said. "Is that your husband's name?"

"My husband's?—No, Madame," she replied. "That is the name of my husband's brother."

"I thought it was Jules. So he told me."

"Ah! Madame does not know him. Jean-Marie

is only a peasant name, and he is ashamed of it, as he is of all his relatives. He is too proud to look at us. I presume Madame is the mother of the young person he has married?"

I replied affirmatively.

"Ah, Madame," resumed Madame Questel; "we were all well pleased when we heard he was going to marry the daughter of the Grand Vizier of Turkey. Who would have thought that the son of a bred and born peasant would ever contract such a fine marriage?"

I felt I was on the threshold of farther revelations, and that all I had to do was to say only just so much as would serve to draw out my new friend.

"Strange!" I remarked.

"And that I should have the honour of calling her sister-in-law, and of receiving in my poor corner so grand a lady as Madame!"

"Oh, I am not a grand lady, Madame," I answered, being desirous of abbreviating her compliments.

"That is because Madame is so good," she resumed, "as to forget her rank to converse with us peasants."

"Pray, Madame," I rejoined, "do not speak in this way. A peasant who earns his bread by the toil of his hands and the sweat of his brow, who is honest and fulfils his duties, is as good as a king who does nothing and lives upon his people. Believe me, I respect labour, and I respect the peasant."

I held out my hand which she seized with earnestness, and pressed it warmly.

"Ah, Madame! If all were only like you. If our Jean-Marie could but see things in the same light. I suppose now he is so rich, we shall see less of him than ever, and he will despise us more. Two hundred thousand francs are a large dowry, Madame, not to reckon the diamonds, and the lands, and the inheritance."

I preserved a passive demeanour, but mentally I opened wide my eyes. What next, I thought.

"You think so?" I remarked.

"But, Madame, so does everybody, and in our poor Brittany such fortunes are rare. It is to be hoped he will now pay off all his debts, and not be obliged to sell his land."

"Are all his farms encumbered then?" I inquired.

"But, Madame, he has no farms. He has only the land immediately surrounding the château, and that is not much. It is a pity he did not leave the old cottage standing instead of mortgaging what he had to build that dungeon-looking place of his.

The house you are in, Madame, was his father's, and is quite good enough for us."

"Still," I observed, pushing my inquiries a step farther, "his land brings him in a revenue."

"What is let of it, Madame, would not keep him," answered Madame Questel: "so, of course, he must do something. What it is we cannot know. He is, we suppose, occupied in Paris, where he stays the best part of his time. But, has he not told Madame all this?"

"Nothing," I answered.

"Oh! Madame, then I have been indiscreet; I ought to have held my peace. He will be furious if he should know this came from me."

I comforted Madame Questel with the assurance that I would not betray her, for which promise she expressed her gratitude. Our conversation was interrupted by the entrance of a bluff, burly man in heavy wooden shoes, a slouch hat, and a smock frock. Madame introduced him to me as her husband, and he saluted me with an air of frankness which impressed me favourably. I could see he was quite in the rough, but he had a pleasant open countenance and an agreeable smile. Unlike his brother, he looked me steadily in the face when speaking, and I could see he was summing me up.

I had yet to go through another ceremony, that of presentation to five robust daughters, the eldest being only ten, and whose cheeks, had they been clean, I would fain have kissed. The family were about to get a meal so I rose to depart, after accepting a cup of milk. Monsieur and Madame Questel hoped I would come again soon and often, and invited me, specially, to a wedding feast to take place within a few days in their neighbourhood, and the date of which they begged me not to forget. I assured them I should not do so, and with this promise took my leave.

We had returned from Paris a month when this revelation was made to me. The effect it produced upon me may more easily be imagined than described. How many more "little secrets" lay behind? It was clear we were duped, but what motive had prompted Questel to deceive us in this manner? Was he looking to a reversion of my daughter's fortune? The issue of our applications to Constantinople was uncertain, and to lay out such a sum of money as our entertainment, our trip to London, and other expenses, must have cost, let alone the taking upon himself the burden of a wife and her mother, all this upon mere speculation, seemed to me to be an act too absurd for a man, evidently so shrewd as Questel, to indulge in. No! There was some deeper reason; but what could it be? On my way home I turned the whole matter over in my mind, and decided to keep my own counsel until the opportunity should present itself for me to disclose my knowledge.

I never learnt whether Questel knew I had evaded his vigilance on that occasion. I am inclined to think he never suspected the fact. If he knew it, his dissimulation was perfect. His manner to me was as polite and deferential as hitherto, and his small courtesies were as punctiliously minute.

On the day appointed for the marriage feast I told my son-in-law I had heard there was to be held a festival of this kind and I should like to witness it. He changed colour and his lips twitched nervously; but in remonstrating with me, as I expected he would do, his voice retained its firmness, and his meekness of manner remained unchanged by the violent emotion to which at that moment he must have been a prey. "Why did I wish to attend such a gathering? A parcel of peasants; low, vulgar, and uneducated people; what was to be gained by associating with such?"

"The novelty of the thing is the great attraction to me," I replied. "I am in a new country, and desire to make myself acquainted with the manners and customs of its people."

"Madame will pardon me if I venture to represent that it is not a place at which it is proper she should be seen."

I objected that Monsieur le Curé would be there no doubt, and many of the small landowners, and there would not be any impropriety in my being present in the midst of such company.

"But Madame knows that I do not care she should mix with the people of this neighbourhood. I do not do so myself."

"You cannot expect," I replied, "that I shall remain always confined within the walls of this house, or to the limits of your garden, and be from year's end to year's end restricted to the sight of your face and those of your domestics! They are agreeable, no doubt, but they are monotonous."

"I have no wish to impose any such restrictions upon Madame," was his answer, in the same low tone, and with the same meek deferential manner. "We shall soon have change enough to satisfy Madame. But so long as we remain here it would be agreeable to me if Madame would conform to my wishes, and not seek to make acquaintances in this neighbourhood of whom, I regret to say, I disapprove. Madame will not go to this fête."

"Madame intends to go," I retorted; for I felt I must now either assert and maintain my independence of action, or surrender myself into the hands of a man, who I perceived was none the less a tyrant for concealing his claws in kid gloves. "Madame is no prisoner, Monsieur Questel," I went on to say; "nor is she a child in leading-strings. Madame has made up her mind to go, and go she assuredly will."

"Madame will, of course, do as she pleases," replied he, with a scarcely perceptible shrug of the shoulders, and with a smile on his now blanched lips which suddenly revealed to me the demon lurking beneath that smooth exterior. "I cannot restrain Madame. But Madame will bear in mind she goes against my express desire, and in the face of my friendly prohibition."

I went to the fête, of course.

My new friends were delighted to see me. They received me with every possible demonstration of welcome. They assigned me the place of honour at the long table in the large field upon which the banquet was spread, consisting of joints of veal of awful solidity; fowls, salads, pies and tarts, and custards; cheese in bulk; galettes—a kind of butter pastry-cake—fruits in mounds; cider and other drinkables in superabundance; to the demolition of all which delicacies the guests, male and female, young and old, addressed themselves with an earnestness of purpose and a capacity for stowage, which were nothing short of marvellous to me; quite unaccustomed to witness such feasting.

My sister-in-law had taken me by the hand and seated me by her side. She helped me, I verily believe, to a portion of everything upon the table, manifestly labouring under the superstition that the cramming of a guest is the culminating point of hospitality. She presented me to everybody, and I found myself overwhelmed in quite a deluge of Questel connexions, to the entire extinction of a possibility of further removes. After the feasting, the satisfied guests took to dancing by way of promoting digestion. The instrument was the *cornemuse*, or *binoui*, a kind of bagpipes, which gives forth its music only under pressure, and revenges itself by yielding, as if by way of protest, a series of most excruciating discords. To join in the exercise it provoked I had no desire, but I found refusal impossible, so importunate were the cavaliers of the family. I gave in, however, only after an assurance from Madame Questel that not to join in the dance would be regarded as an indication of pride on my part, and would produce an unfavourable impression. I could take one turn or two and then retire. Thus admonished, I surrendered myself into the power of a herculean Questel to be hustled and pushed, and bumped, and dragged, and whirled, and pulled about after a fashion which, in the shape of bruises and tender bones, left me something to remember for many days. Having undergone my penance, I resumed my seat, far less delighted than the amiable monster to whom I remain indebted for the most awful shaking I ever got in my life.

I thoroughly enjoyed the plain, straight-forward ways of my new friends, and remained with them until seven in the evening, Monsieur conducting me a good distance on my way home. I was informed, before I left, that a relative would shortly be married, and to that festival I must promise to come, and to bring my daughter. This I consented to do, immensely to the gratification of those who invited me.

Ayesha, being indisposed, had retired when I reached home. I found my son-in-law quite ready to receive me, and, as usual, he was prodigal of his small attentions. In spite of his placid exterior, I knew he must be in a terrible state of mental fret, but I had resolved not to betray his sister-in-law's confidence, nor to reveal what I had learnt until my own time came for doing so. When, therefore, placing my footstool—as was his custom—under my feet, he inquired blandly and with an air of infinite unconcern, what I had seen, I merely answered that I had witnessed a very curious festival, and passed a very agreeable day.

"And the—the peasants, Madame," he added, with a marked contemptuous emphasis upon the word.

"Very pleasant people," I replied. "Plain, rough, even uncouth, but to all appearance, frank and hospitable. I rather like them. They seemed rather proud, than otherwise, of their independent position as cultivators of the soil."

"Nothing much to be proud of," ejaculated he.

"Nothing to be ashamed of," I answered. "A man who is peasant born should not blush to acknowledge it."

Questel made no reply, but I saw plainly enough my bolt had struck home. Probably, either suspecting I had learnt far more concerning him than he wished me to know, or, perhaps, doubtful of the extent of my knowledge, and fearful of provoking a disclosure inopportunely, he did not push the conversation any further, but allowed me to retire on the plea of my feeling over-fatigued, which, in fact, was the case.

I think he must have passed an uncomfortable night.

CHAPTER X.

I impart to Ayesha her husband's history—We are invited to a family festival—A domestic crisis—More revelations—I have an explanation with my son-in-law.

I took the very earliest opportunity next day to ascertain of Ayesha whether her husband had acquainted her with any new facts relating to himself and family. He had not. It therefore became my painful duty to make her as wise as myself, but the disclosure did not appear to affect her very much. We had been duped, it was true; but she had at least a protector, bound to provide for her and for me; and this was preferable to a fitful life of plenty and poverty; to alternations of hope and despair. Her husband must now take the necessary steps for the recovery of her property, which, once obtained, would suffice for all.

Although I deemed it my duty to disclose to Ayesha the secret I had discovered, I did not consider myself justified in commenting upon her husband's duplicity. I felt that Ayesha might justly remind me of her aversion to the marriage and of my having promoted it. Nor would it have been right on my part to excite her against him by imparting the thoughts which gave me so much uneasiness, and which were fixed upon determining, if possible, what deep design had to be carried out through our instrumentality; for, that mischief was afoot I did not now entertain the slightest doubt. That mysterious man in the garden, and the transfer of the money-bags to Questel, haunted me like a spectre. Could he be a spy? Had the Ottoman Embassy anything to do with this strange business? Had Questel derived funds from that quarter to make a show and impose upon us, in order to establish a control over us? This point I could not determine, but my convictions began to tend very strongly in that direction.

My description of the festival highly entertained Ayesha. I informed her of the projected one, and of the conditional promise I had made to take her to it. She was delighted, and especially at the prospect of making acquaintance with her new relatives. We agreed no mention should be made to her husband of our intention, nor of the information I had obtained concerning him. It was well to be warned and on our guard; but, as we could not help ourselves, to wait was our only alternative.

All this time no news came from Constantinople!

Some days after this conversation with my daughter, a visitor to us was announced. Questel had gone out. It was the Mayor of the neighbouring village, where the forthcoming wedding-festival was to take place next day, and he came formally to invite our attendance. As we had made up our mind to go, we dismissed this worthy functionary with the assurance which—as he begged us to believe—he only required to make him supremely happy; and in this state of mind he took his departure.

On Questel's return, Ayesha, in high glee, informed him of our acceptance of this invitation; and expressing her delight at the prospect of seeing a new phase of French country life, and of being introduced to his relatives, added, that, with him by her side, she anticipated passing a very happy day. To her astonishment, but not to mine, he replied abruptly:

"I shall not go, nor shall you. Your mother may do so if she pleases, as she has already placed herself in opposition to my wish that she should not visit the people in this neighbourhood; but you—you shall not go."

The suddenness of the refusal, his peremptory tone, his excited manner, for the moment startled Ayesha. She stood for a few seconds looking into his changed countenance—for his face and lips had turned white—as though unable to realize that he was the same man whose indulgence, kindness, and meekness had hitherto been so uniform. But her hesitation did not last long. Her flashing eyes and heightened colour indicated the coming storm, which she nevertheless struggled to suppress.

"I shall not go?" she presently said, her burning glance turned full upon him.

"You shall not," was his steady reply.

"You prohibit me accompanying my mother?" she asked.

"Formally and decidedly," he rejoined.

"Then, Monsieur," she exclaimed, "I tell you I will go. What reasons can you have for seeking to prevent me and my mother from taking a little recreation? Why should you object to our visiting your relatives, who are now ours, and from showing them civilities in return? Tell me that."

"I have no explanations to give to you,

Madame," he retorted. "I have reasons. They are my own, and that is sufficient."

"No, Monsieur," she continued, "that is not sufficient. I know the reasons. Yes! You may open your eyes, but I repeat it: I know your reasons. They are of no value now. You cannot have anything more to conceal from us."

"I demand an explanation," he exclaimed, trembling with rage and mortification. "Your mother has been exciting you to rebel against my authority —to defy it in fact."

"My mother has done no such thing, Monsieur. My mother knows herself too well to condescend to such a meanness. It is I, of my own accord, who rebel against an authority so unjustly and so absurdly asserted. Yes, Monsieur; and in this instance I defy it, as I will whenever you attempt to place it between me and an innocent, legitimate indulgence. I tell you we cannot learn of you more than we know."

"Again, Madame," he now vociferated, "I demand an explanation! What do you know?"

"More, Monsieur, than you cared to tell us three months ago, more than I care to repeat. We know everything. Let that suffice for you."

How far this altercation might have proceeded,

or to what result it might have led, but for my interference, I know not.

"We had far better drop the matter of explanation, Monsieur Questel," I said. "No good can come of it. We have no wish to defy your authority; but, on the other hand, you must not expect us to consent to be kept close prisoners in this château. We shall go to this family festival, and you will be reasonable and accompany us. It will be best for all parties."

"It would be far more reasonable for none of us to go," he answered, after a pause, during which he walked a few paces to and fro in the room, and which produced the effect of a counter-irritant. "At any rate, I can think of it. But I warn you, I will be master in my own house."

With this, he abruptly quitted the apartment, leaving Ayesha and me to our reflections.

From that hour Monsieur Questel's attentions to me began to decline.

Next forenoon M. Questel, who had not referred to the scene of the preceding day, seeing we were preparing to depart, put on his hat as soon as we were ready, and, without saying a word, proceeded with us to the place of meeting. Our arrival was the second great event of the day. Of course the Questels mustered in force, and I shall not soon forget the discomfiture of my son-in-law when he found himself obliged to acknowledge his relatives. It was absolutely pitiable to witness him writhing under the tortures of his wounded vanity. He took an early opportunity of abandoning the field, although he kept somewhere near, for he continually appeared and disappeared, never remaining long present or absent. He did not sit down to dinner, nor take part in the gaieties that succeeded it. Why he came at all, unless to watch us, seeing he would neither eat, drink, nor be sociable, puzzled me exceedingly.

The repast was on pretty much the same solid scale as the one I had last attended. After it, the Mayor, who occupied the seat of honour next the bride, came up to me, and, with a profound obeisance, said:

"Madame, I am very happy to have the honour of renewing my acquaintance with you. Madame, probably, does not forget me. I am the Mayor of the village, and I hope you will favour me with the honour of a call. I shall be delighted to see you. I keep a little chandler's shop, Madame, and whenever you require anything in my line—

sugar, pepper, matches, mustard, coffee, candles, soap—I have a good stock, and shall be very happy to supply you. I used to be very intimate with your son-in-law, Madame, but he is so proud now he will not speak to me."

The warning groans of the bagpipes very fortunately interrupted the conversation, and brought in a considerable number of other guests, of whom some forty arranged themselves in a ring in the meadow—all joining hands—and began a whirligig dance, going round and round, and keeping time by stamping on the ground with their wooden shoes. I looked on, amused enough, but was not left long to this enjoyment, for a laughing, ruddy-faced youth took forcible possession of me, in spite of my protest that I was too old to dance, and made me take two or three turns, when, on my telling him I felt tired, he very politely conducted me to my seat. Fortunately my swain belonged to the category of gentle ones, and my second saltatory experiment in these parts did not leave me with bruised flesh and tender bones.

The Breton costume for men and women is characteristic and striking enough, but close inspection robs it of half its charm. The men wear a broad-brimmed, slouch hat, a kind of round jacket—when it is not a smock-frock—baggy trowsers gathered in above the knee and falling over it—but not so as to conceal the calf of the leg—and sabots on the feet. Very many of the young men wore their hair flowing down over their shoulders and back, but cut off straight across the forehead. The women also wear wooden shoes, a close-fitting bodice, a short skirt of woollen stuff or other material, with aprons, having two pockets in them, and on their head a skull-cap having a deep, plaited border, like the coif of a nun. The bride's dress was of the same fashion, only of some dark-coloured silk. Her cap had a flower in it, and she wore a nosegay in her waistband.

As may be imagined, Ayesha's appearance at this fête caused the liveliest sensation. In Brittany the spirit of feudalism yet lingers, and respect for superior rank is still a sentiment, like loyalty. The clergy and the aristocracy are real powers in that province, and their representatives are absolutely small potentates. These facts will explain the sort of awe with which Ayesha was at first regarded. It appeared to me that they looked upon her—a real, native-born Turk, as a sort of *lusus naturæ*—a natural curiosity, to be examined from all sides, to be inspected at every turn. Some remained content to stand and stare at her from a distance, making their comments in under-tones to one another. Others came prowling inquisitively around her, then gradually ventured to cluster nearer to her, whilst a few of the boldest presently advanced to salute her and to address her a few compliments. At all this Ayesha was immensely amused, but she soon placed herself upon a good footing with her new friends, and as everything was novel, she entered fully into the spirit of the scene, and enjoyed herself thoroughly.

It will be conjectured that I did not lose the opportunity this fête afforded me of learning what more I could concerning M. Questel, and his affairs. My sister-in-law was my chief informant.

"Why don't you come to the château sometimes?" I asked.

"Because, Madame," she replied, "Jean-Marie is too proud for us. You see, he is very ambitious. Now, we are contented and happy in our position. We work for our living, but we have everything we want; we live very comfortably, and we put by money."

"By-the-by," said I, "you told me the other day that your brother-in-law had debts."

"Yes, Madame!" she answered. "Before he

went to Paris he owed forty thousand francs, and when it was settled that he should marry your daughter, he borrowed ten thousand more of a notary at Vannes. But then, you see, even fifty thousand francs, though it is a large sum, can well be spared out of two hundred thousand, and leave something handsome to live upon. My husband and I were glad to hear that Jean-Marie had married a lady with such a handsome dowry, and expectations besides."

"I think you also told me," I rejoined, "that your brother-in-law's income was small?"

"Only three hundred francs a month, Madame. How can he live upon that? The interest upon his debts would nearly swallow up the whole."

"Well," I said, "now, as you remarked the other day, he will be able to pay his debts. I am sorry you are not friends. You must come to the château and see us."

"Ah! Madame, we should wish to do so, but we are all afraid of Jean-Marie. He is so violent. His temper is horrible. He despises us, and I and my husband are naturally very angry with him. You saw him to-day. He would scarcely recognise us."

I renewed my invitation, notwithstanding, to Madame and her husband to pay me a visit at the château, and quietly took my leave somewhat early, as Monsieur Questel had not re-appeared for a considerable time. I had reason to believe, however, that he was at no great distance from us; in fact, he arrived almost immediately after we reached the house.

I was not displeased at the absence of his usual attentions that evening, and withdrew much earlier than my habitual hour to study the position and to decide upon a course.

After breakfast next morning, I intimated my wish to speak to him alone. I went out into the garden. He followed me.

"Monsieur Questel," said I, after we had proceeded a few paces, "you will not be surprised that, after the occurrences of the last few days, I should seek to have some conversation with you."

"I listen to you, Madame," was his curt reply.

"In the first place, when by the merest accident I discovered that your brother and his wife lived close by, I was greatly surprised you never told me they were such near neighbours. I was glad to make their acquaintance, and I like them very much."

He bowed slightly, but said nothing.

"You have been extremely careful, also, to keep

us in total ignorance of the position of your family, who are honest peasants, of whom you are ashamed, though you are yourself a peasant's son."

Still he made no reply.

"You told me, Monsieur, that your mother was alive, in London, living on her income, and belonged to a very high family. Why did you invent such an infamous falsehood?"

He was very pale, but held his peace.

"You knew, Monsieur, that she was dead. There was no necessity to tell me an untruth about her. My daughter is not at all fond of mothers-in-law."

"Madame," he retorted, "your daughter is not singular in this respect."

I would not notice this sarcasm. I had my own purpose to pursue, and it was indispensable he should hear me to the end.

"You have grossly, designedly deceived us, Monsieur Questel," I resumed. "When you saw us in our sad state in Paris, we had not sought you. It was you who came to us. We were not seeking for grandeur nor riches. We wanted only tranquillity and a peaceful home. We found in the one to which you brought us, luxury, extravagance, prodigal expenditure, wholly unjustifiable in a man owing forty thousand francs at that very time, and whose entire income, upon which he could depend, amounted to only three hundred francs a month."

"Madame has been very minutely informed," he answered, a malicious smile distorting his mouth. "Pray continue."

"You increased that debt, Monsieur," I continued, "by borrowing ten thousand more of a notary at Vannes, upon the strength of my daughter's acceptance of you for her husband; and you gave out that she would bring you a dowry of two hundred thousand francs, besides what she would inherit from her father; another vile and detestable falsehood, the object of it being to deceive us as to the extent of your means, in furtherance of some design of your own, in which I cannot avoid the conviction that we are intended to play no subordinate part. Is this not so?"

"I have no reply to make to such a question," he answered. "Madame forms her convictions independently of me."

"Monsieur," I resumed, "it is not my object to waste words in exposing what you know are mere evasions. I take it for granted you have such a design in your mind. You will not tell me what it is; a sign that it cannot be a good one. But we are wholly at your mercy, and must abide events, trusting to Providence to protect us from harm. In the meantime, Monsieur, things here cannot go on as they are."

"At last!" he exclaimed. "We are then coming to something."

"Monsieur," said I, "the past cannot be recalled, but the errors belonging to it can be remedied. You are my son-in-law now, and it is my duty to take an interest in your affairs. Now, listen to me. Our present scale of living must be reduced. You must not incur any more debts on our account, nor run into needless expenses. The more simply we live the better; and in the first place, I recommend you to discharge at once, our waiting-maid and your man-servant. I will undertake the management of your household concerns, and you need not, in fact, keep more than one domestic. Say, shall this be so?"

We walked on a few yards further in silence, when he said:

"As it seems I cannot be master in my own house, I may as well relinquish the future direction of it into Madame's hands. From to-morrow, Madame is free to act as she pleases. Has Madame anything more to say to me?"

"Not at present, Monsieur."

"Then I beg, respectfully, to wish Madame good morning," he retorted; and turning on his heel he walked rapidly away, leaving me to return home alone.

CHAPTER XI.

M. Questel's ill-treatment of me—Ayesha in terror—Violent scenes at home—M. Questel throws off the mask—The plot against myself and Ayesha revealed.

I soon found that in acceding to the request I had preferred, in his interests, Monsieur Questel had in view the rendering of my life as miserable as possible. He held the purse-strings, and from being profuse became niggardly. I remembered that this was the character given to me of him some short time back, but the description fell short of the reality. He cavilled at the minutest expenditure, urging my recommendation that we must live economically. He grew every day more intractable, more exacting, more dissatisfied. The common necessaries were grudged us, and we never sat down to a meal but a lecture on my extravagance accompanied it. We had discharged those domestics whom I regarded as unnecessary appendages, remaining with only one. One day she also disappeared without previous notice to me, and upon my inquiring what had become of her, Monsieur informed me he had dismissed her; sent her away on the moment, as he could no longer afford to keep even one servant.

From that day I became the household drudge.

Ayesha beheld all this without emotion. She seemed to have subsided into a condition of apathy, out of which she could not, or would not, be roused. She had come to entertain a sort of liking for her husband, or, at any rate, professed a kindling of affection for him at the very time his treatment of us—of me especially—ought to have disentitled him to the smallest regard or consideration. She admitted his duplicity, his brutality, his penuriousness, his evil disposition; but in answer to my suggestions to seek with me a remedy in flight, replied placidly, that she must resign herself to her fate, and as Providence had given her a second bad husband, she had no alternative but to put up with him.

I had already made so many sacrifices for my daughter, that to remain by her, under these circumstances, seemed to me an imperative duty, suffer what I might. Then, maternal affection suggested an instinctive conviction that she was in imminent personal peril. It took fast hold of my mind and confirmed my views of my present duty. Soon the suspicion began gradually to dawn upon me, that her husband had discovered or invented some means of terrorizing her, and hence this unnatural submissiveness on her part. I felt satisfied this tension could not last long. Studying her hourly, from day to day, I came to the conclusion that her moral enervation originated in absolute despair of any immediate remedy for the actual state of things, and isolated as she now was from elevating influences of every kind, I could see and deplore that the want of education, leaving her wholly without mental resources, threw her back upon a nature, blunted to the higher moral sentiments by the debasing associations of her early life. In this way only could I account for her outward indifference to the humiliations I was forced to endure, and to the degradation to which I was reduced.

During the spring Monsieur Questel fell ill of a rheumatic complaint of a chronic character. Unable to move without suffering intense pain, he became a very demon. His impatience and irritability degenerated into absolute fury. He raved, and stormed, and swore, and cursed day and night.

Nothing satisfied him. We waited upon him—or it were more accurate to say I did—almost without intermission. There was no hand but mine to prepare his food, to make his drinks, to attend to his wants of every kind. Everything had to be conveyed to him up four flights of stairs, and he would often summon me on the most trivial pretext a few minutes after I had left his chamber. In my own individual capacity I discharged the multifarious functions of housekeeper, cook, housemaid, washerwoman, laundress, and hospital nurse; and, last of all, I had to undertake the office of gardener, and dig and sow, and plant, and gather. Had we retained our horses, I should probably have had to act as groom and stableman.

Convalescence not only brought no respite, but even aggravated the situation. His demands upon me were more exacting, his fits of impatience more furious, his paroxysms of anger scarcely intermittent. He knew we were wholly in his power, defenceless, without resources, obliged to endure his brutal insolence, and he now never any day failed to assail us with reproaches that we were a burden to him, to which he would occasionally add an intimation that it would soon end. How, nor in what manner, we could neither know nor foresee.

This miserable existence had lasted about three months, when, one day, Ayesha having gone into the garden with her husband, I heard her scream. I rushed out, and saw him dragging her brutally along by her wrists, towards the house. He loosed his hold of her on perceiving me, and Ayesha ran into my arms.

"What is the meaning of this?" I asked.

"He wanted to prevent me from going to my brother-in-law," Ayesha replied, sobbing.

"What do you want with him, my child?"

"Mamma, it was to claim his protection. I can't bear it any longer!"

"Bear what, my child?"

"He threatens to take me to Constantinople, mamma dear, and I won't go. I would rather die. He has been threatening to do so for months, unless I would remain passive and do absolutely what he wished. But I can't bear it any longer. Go to Constantinople I will not, come what may."

The sight of my daughter struggling in the hands of this ruffian in kid gloves, so excited and bewildered me, I gave no heed to him; and when, after embracing her, I looked up, he had disappeared.

"To Constantinople!" I exclaimed. "What treachery is afoot now? No, my child! You shall not be taken back to Constantinople against your will, so long as I am by to prevent it."

I had enough food for reflection that night.

"To Constantinople!" The threat of taking her to that hated place was then, the means he had employed to terrify her. I felt certain that whatever else might happen, she would not return to Constantinople. But why this threat? What mystery did it cover?

Not many days elapsed before another and more violent scene ensued. It arose out of my requesting to be supplied with the means of purchasing necessaries; a certain provocative of fury on his part, under any circumstances.

"You are always wanting money," he said. "You know I have none, or very little."

"But we must have food," I retorted. "Our living, compared with what it was, does not cost you much, Monsieur Questel."

"I don't see why I should provide food for either of you!" was his brutal reply; "you especially, Madame!" he added, looking at me vindictively.

"I am earning the little you give me, Monsieur," I responded. "I am your servant, only without wages. Your wife, my daughter, you are bound to maintain."

"I tell you, then," he said, "I will not spend any more money on you. Why don't you go back to Constantinople, both of you? There you have money. You can have as much as you want. Why don't you get it? Why do you live on me?"

"We are not living on you, Monsieur," I answered. "I repeat, that I more than earn my morsel, and your wife you must keep. I have been your servant, your house-drudge, your slave, and have endured your brutality and your insolence, and every kind of humiliation on account of my daughter, whom I would not, nay, will not, abandon to your savage mercy."

"And what should I care, pray, Madame, for the divorced wife of a Turk?" he retorted, now livid with rage, and trembling in every limb. "I am not a Minister!" Then, turning to his wife, he continued; "I have no money for such as you, Madame. Do you think I married you for your beauty? Bah!"

"You insolent ruffian!" I cried, my own blood in a boil. "How dare you insult my daughter in this vile manner? She did not seek to marry you! You sought her hand; and why, pray, if not for herself, since you knew well she had no money?"

"Ah!" he exclaimed; "you challenge me to answer that! You want my secret, do you? Well, then, I throw off my mask now, and you shall know. *Parbleu!* Why did I marry her unless it was for money?"

I repeated the word. I and Ayesha stood aghast.

"Yes, money!" he retorted. "I prefer that to beauty!" Here he again addressed my daughter: "Yes, Madame, for your money I married you, not for your beauty!"

"But I have no money!" exclaimed Ayesha.

"Ah, no? But your father is a Minister! He is rich. He wants you back in Constantinople, and —what, you don't know—he has offered a reward of two hundred thousand francs to whoever shall deliver you up to him, that he may cherish and take care of you! Yes, Madame, and I—I will take you to him, and get that money! I will turn Mahometan, and the Pasha will get me a place. I will be a Consul, or a State Secretary, or a Chargé d'Affaires! He won't be able to refuse me. I am not bound to keep Kibrizli's wife and child. Here in France it is the custom for a wife to bring a dowry to her husband. How could you be such an imbecile as to think I should take you without a franc, without education, and half stupid, unless I expected to be well compensated? I won't support you any longer in France. I will go to Constantinople, I tell you, and I will make you go!"

"Not while I live and can defend her from your vile and crafty designs!" I exclaimed, suddenly interrupting him at this point of his voluble and audacious tirade. "I will not allow you to talk— to speak, to her in this way: at least, in my presence! I see now exactly what you are! Your own infamous, cowardly language, betrays you! I ought to have believed what others told me about you! I now see you desired to rid yourself of me that you might obtain the control over my daughter; but, although she is your wife, you shall not do with her as you like, for you are a cheat and a bad man, and I will not leave her; and, Monsieur Questel— Monsieur Jean-Marie Questel—she shall not go back to Constantinople!"

"And I tell you, Madame," retorted he, gesticulating furiously, "that she shall go! She shall go back, Madame! I swear it, Madame! She shall go! she shall!"

Unable to restrain himself, he tore out of the room, mad with fury, disappointment, and mortification, and reiterating his last assertion with an oath that made my blood curdle.

I summed up the situation: Ayesha was incapable of thought. Here were, to my apprehension, the simple facts, after the clean breast of it Monsieur Questel had made.

Persistent silence on the part of my husband, to reduce us to submission from actual want! Failure of this design! A new plot! A reward of two hundred thousand francs offered for our re-capture and safe delivery into the hands of the Pasha! A secret spy, in the pay of the Ottoman Embassy, employed to introduce a pauperised, penniless, intriguing villain, to undertake the infamous, detestable task of betraying us! Funds furnished by my husband's agents to enable the vile instrument to impose upon us by a fictitious display of wealth, and thus disarm suspicion and lead us into the snare craftily laid for us! The return to the château, and the indignities to which I was subjected, a part of Questel's astute plan to excite my disgust and force me to leave Ayesha in his hands! Ayesha, his wife, compelled to follow him: at least, so went the calculation! Her marriage with the Giaour not recognised in Turkey; a divorce; the thirty pieces of silver paid to the Judas Iscariot;

Ayesha delivered over to the Pasha; Questel rich —for France; and I—I? I! Well—what mattered what became of me?

It may be imagined, after such a scene as I have described—though no words of mine can possibly convey an accurate idea of it in its details—that I avoided my son-in-law as much as possible; and as he did not manifest the least eagerness to encounter me, the truce suited both of us.

But he had not yet gone to the extreme limit of his deliberate scheme of persecution of me. He now forbade intercourse between me and Ayesha, knowing that to see her, to caress her, were my sole pleasure. We could only speak to each other by stealth, as he was continually on the watch. If I did not defy his prohibition it was solely because I feared his violence might be turned against my daughter, and her life be placed in peril, for I now believed him capable of any atrocity.

Yet what could I do, but wait and watch?

CHAPTER XII.

Further mystery at the Château de Kerbeque—Fresh revelations concerning my son-in-law—His projects and counter-projects—We return to Paris.

My worst suspicions being now confirmed, and my vigilance thoroughly awakened, I scarcely rested night nor day. It was certain, after disclosing the infamous conspiracy for our recapture, in which he played so important a part, that Questel would hasten to bring matters to an issue. Indeed, I entertained no doubt that issue was proximate, or he would have retained his mask a little longer.

I arrived at this conclusion from noticing daily incidents. The postman suddenly discontinued bringing letters to the house. He was a paid spy of Questel's, though I was not aware of the fact at the time. His office came to be discharged by the woman to whom I have already referred as the landlady of the small wine-shop and restaurant where I had first made inquiry concerning Questel, and who, I ascertained later, had formerly stood towards him in the relation of mistress. She now also acted as one of his spies and as temporary postman, for reasons Monsieur Questel knew better than I. Sometimes this woman would bring the letters whilst we were at breakfast. On one particular occasion I observed her hand him one bearing the Constantinople post-mark. He at once concealed it, but I could see, by the expression of his countenance, that the communication was a welcome one. I was determined he should know I was aware whence the letter came.

"So you have correspondence with Constantinople?" said I.

He looked at me fiercely, and in the sharpest of tones retorted :

"What is that to you, whether I have or not?"

"Oh, only that it gives me room to hazard a suspicion respecting your correspondents," was my reply.

He made no answer, but went out of the room. This, however, was the last time the woman officiated as letter-carrier.

Monsieur Questel now daily grew more uneasy and anxious as the hour came round for the appearance of the postman, for whom he would watch impatiently. Sometimes he took him into his own room, where the two would remain closeted for a considerable time. Monsieur Questel's correspondence also increased daily, and he went frequently to Vannes, between which place and the château, messengers passed to and fro frequently. I may add, that, through his spy, the regular letter-carrier, Monsieur Questel was kept posted up whenever I wrote to anyone.

I knew all these mysterious proceedings boded us no good, but I also felt they were bringing matters to a crisis.

I had entirely emancipated myself by this time from the restraints upon my personal liberty which Monsieur Questel had sought to impose, and my excursions in the neighbourhood were not confined to his relatives. My anxiety became daily less supportable, but no one could offer me any relief.

One day, in a despairing mood, I sought the Curé. I had not been able to speak to Ayesha for several days, and so closely had he watched us that I was reduced to the last shifts for the opportunity of saying a word to her. If I saw her alone, I would rush by, and hastily mutter a caution to her as I passed; yet not always did I succeed in evading the vigilance of Questel, who would suddenly dart upon Ayesha, and demand to know what I had said. I thought the Curé might, perhaps, advise me what to do under such trying circumstances.

The reverend father deeply commiserated me, but told me candidly, though in the kindest terms, that I had been to blame in not seeking him out at first. The character he gave of my son-in-law coincided with my own sad experience of him. He was simply detested in his own neighbourhood for his pride and avarice, and had become its laughing-stock since he had mounted the fez. He had avowed his intention of turning Mahometan, which, it was added, signified very little, as he had long since declared himself an infidel. As to his means of existence, beyond the small sum he derived from the rent of his land, he was known to be in the service of the secret police: he was in fact, a *mouchard*. The Curé pitied Ayesha, but as she preferred to remain with such a man, my sole remedy for my own troubles and daily trials was to leave her and return to Paris.

I had already thought of doing this, but only at the last extremity.

I received the same advice from Questel's brother, and from other of his relatives. None spoke well of him, and all wondered how he should have succeeded in deceiving me as to his position and his means. His cousin, an *avocat* at Vannes, told me Questel's avowed purpose was to take back his wife to Constantinople, for that he looked to the two hundred thousand francs her father had promised to whomsoever should " restore her to his love," as the sole source whence to satisfy his numerous creditors, who now threatened to sell him up. The cousin could not see any other way for me to avoid further trials than a return to Paris, leaving Ayesha behind. But I was not prepared to do this yet.

The fact is, Monsieur Questel had begun to throw out dark hints of some impending change. He no longer, or but seldom, talked of going to Constantinople, but of disposing of his property, and taking a journey round the world; then it was a trip to Marseilles he thought of making, or to Bordeaux, or to some other port. He daily altered his project, or pretended to do so, to baffle me, I strongly suspected; but to my mind one thing was certain : he contemplated a move of some kind, and I was not deceived by his apparent irresolution. I felt certain Constantinople was his real objective point.

I also learnt from Ayesha—for despite his lynx-eyed watchfulness we now and then contrived to exchange a few words—that he was pressing her to give him her procuration, in order to enable him to claim her property, in the event of her persisting in not accompanying him to Constantinople. This Ayesha declared to me she would not do on any account. She would go with him to Paris, but no power on earth should compel her to trust herself alone with him in a strange port. If he succeeded by force in conveying her on board any vessel, or in inveigling her to it, she vowed she would resist to the last extremity, and if driven to a desperate remedy, would throw herself overboard; and I knew she would be as good as her word.

Ayesha's experience of the world amounted to that of the merest child. She was—I must tell the truth—absolutely stupid in this respect; but, her mind once made up on any point, right or wrong, she was not to be moved. I learnt that she had had of late numerous contentions with her husband on the score of the journeys he hinted she would be forced to take with him, and that she had told him of her resolution not to trust herself to go with him elsewhere than to Paris unless I accompanied her. I believe he had acquired sufficient experience of her stubbornness of will to teach him the wisdom of not putting it to the test.

One morning, Monsieur Questel referred, of his

own accord, to the continued absence of any communication from Constantinople concerning my affairs, and intimated the desirability of our endeavouring to ascertain something about them. I concluded it was not any special interest in my matters which prompted my astute son-in-law to throw out this suggestion, but it did not suit my purpose to contradict him. I knew that the Abbé Boré would have communicated with me, had any intelligence reached him from my husband, and Monsieur Questel knew this as well as I did. When, therefore, he presently expressed the opinion that a visit to Paris might be necessary, I understood he had already made up his mind to go thither. This proved to be the case, greatly to my own and Ayesha's delight.

CHAPTER XIII.

A disclosure relating to Ayesha's marriage—Monsieur Questel refuses to have it legalised—A visit to the Procureur Impérial with the Princess Davidoff—The result.

ONE of my earliest visits was to our dear friend the Abbé Boré, to whom I related the occurrences of the last few months. He rebuked me in kind terms for not confiding in him from the commencement of our acquaintance with Monsieur Questel, as inquiries could have been set on foot to ascertain his position and his antecedents. It was now too late to interfere, but further mischief might be guarded against.

His first warning related to my daughter's marriage. I had seen the certificate only twice. The first time Ayesha had herself shown it to me. It was on her return from London after the ceremony. The second time was on the present occasion, when Ayesha entrusted me with it to show to our friend. The Abbé at once pointed out to me a fact, my ignorance of which was attributable to my lack of knowledge of the English language. The marriage had been solemnised in an English Protestant Church, and, necessarily, according to the forms of that establishment. He explained to me that the French law did not recognise as valid a marriage contracted under such circumstances, both parties being Catholics. He even expressed the gravest doubt whether the marriage would be held legal in England. In France the civil contract alone bound. It would be indispensable, in order to legalise the marriage for France, to renew it in due form, both civilly and religiously, at the *mairie*, and at church.

Here was another revelation! Here was another act of treachery, and of still deeper dye! This marriage was a mere form: in fact, a farce! In view of the reward of two hundred thousand francs, Questel had schemed only for the means of obtaining them. To give him a claim to legal control over Ayesha, a marriage was necessary. On the other hand, this ceremony would saddle him with an incumbrance in the shape of a wife; and he had avowed he cared only for money. To marry in France, then, presented obvious inconveniences, for although the law would give him legal control over his wife, it would also give her a right to her own property in the absence of any cession of it to him on her part. Anxious only for this legal right of controlling Ayesha's movements, the question for him to decide had been how to secure it yet leave him free—once his end obtained—to repudiate her legally on some plausible and sure ground. A marriage in England, according to the forms of the Protestant church, was the diabolical alternative. If he went to Constantinople, his marriage would stand annulled by the simple fact of her having married a Christian. On this side, therefore, he was safe. In France he could appeal to the law, declare the marriage null and void, and with his two hundred thousand francs in his pocket, laugh at all attempts to make him contribute to the support of her he had betrayed, in the event of her claiming a maintenance of him as her husband.

Truly Monsieur Questel had well considered every contingency which his wisdom had suggested as likely to occur; but he had not included in his estimate of adverse chances, my vigilance and Ayesha's self-will, coupled with her resolution not to return to Constantinople.

It was imperative to rescue Ayesha, without loss of time, from the equivocal position in which the treachery of Questel had placed her, and at the same time to avoid exciting his suspicions. Without giving him the slightest reason to suspect that I saw through the trick of a marriage, ostensibly legal in form but illegal in fact, I represented that the Abbé Boré considered it highly improper this marriage had not been legalised in France, and insisted that it must be done, in order to place her in her right position in society. Questel at once began, as I fully expected he would do, to suggest a number of pretexts for evading this ceremony. He did not see the utility of it. One marriage, no matter where, how, or by whom performed, was as good as twenty. It was a great annoyance to him to be compelled to advertise his name and designation on the door-posts of the *mairie* of his *arrondissement* for the space of three weeks, and to let all the world know he was about to re-marry the woman who was already his wife. Then he did not want the Abbé Boré to know that he, Questel, was peasant-born, which the exhibition of his baptismal certificate would show. Be married again, indeed! No! he would not. He would never consent to go through such a farce.

I had foreseen this contingency, and had prepared myself for it, my fixed purpose being to put Ayesha in the position to which she had a right. Irrespective of consequences this had to be done. Having, therefore, heard my crafty son-in-law to the end, I submitted that in case he persisted in his refusal, means would have to be taken to assert the invalidity of any document Ayesha might sign, under actual circumstances, by raising the question of the legality of her marriage, she having no *status* as a wife according to French law.

I had in my mind the procuration he was endeavouring to obtain, and felt convinced of the effect such an intimation would produce. I was not mistaken. A scarcely perceptible change in the expression of his countenance satisfied me his cupidity had taken the alarm. He hesitated a moment, looking uneasily at me, then blurted out that, of course, if the French law did not recognise the validity of the marriage, there was no alternative but to take the necessary steps to legalise it; for her own sake this ought to be done; he did not wish, of course, that his wife should be considered as holding an equivocal position, but he was not aware she had been placed in it by the celebration of their marriage in an English Protestant church. To one thing, however, he had made up his mind; he would not renew the religious ceremony, and the posting of his name and designation at the doors of the *mairie* must be dispensed with.

I endeavoured to reason him out of this resolution, pointing out that unless he went through the civil forms required by law, the marriage would not be fully legalised. The renewal of the religious ceremony might be dispensed with, but compliance with the municipal regulations was essential.

I could not move him. He asserted that the difficulty could be got over. He knew of cases in point. If the thing had been done for others, it could be done for him.

In this dilemma I had recourse to the Mayor of the ward, who assured me that he durst not and could not dispense with the customary forms. In certain rare instances, a special dispensation from the Procureur Impérial had been accorded, but it was entirely out of the question to suppose that such a departure from the ordinary course would be sanctioned when no valid reason, not even a plausible one, could be urged to justify it.

I did not believe Monsieur Questel's assertion that exemption from compliance with the forms of law, in such cases as his, had been granted under particular circumstances, but I now heard the fact confirmed by authority. The mention of the

Procureur Impérial gave me a new idea and a new hope. He, then, was the personage holding the power that could over-ride the law at a very tight pinch. Was he accessible?

I took the earliest opportunity of conferring with the Princess Davidoff, whom I knew was on a good footing with all the public functionaries and notabilities of the day. Seeing my anxiety, and appreciating the cause of it, she at once most kindly consented to accompany me to the office of the Procureur Impérial, and fixed the day for the visit.

This great legal dignitary appeared, at first, not over pleased at our intrusion into his august presence. But my friend was dressed in a style becoming her rank and means, and had a grand, imposing manner. I presume the two produced an effect, which was enhanced when she announced herself by her own title, and begged the honour of presenting "Her Highness the Princess Kibrizli-Mehemet-Pasha."

I verily thought I should have sunk into the earth on hearing myself thus designated. I could have done so with joy, to conceal my mortification and embarrassment, for, the consciousness of being attired in the very homeliest of apparel, very far indeed from new, was to me most painful under the circumstances. The worn places in my dress suddenly came out with awful distinctness. I had never before noticed how rusty my shoes were, how sadly my gloves needed mending with a new pair. A Princess in rags! How I contrived to make my obeisance to the grand personage whose attention had been thus so specially directed to me, I know not. I observed him eyeing me inquisitively from head to foot, with an air which indicated a suspicion on his part of being hoaxed; and, notwithstanding the courteous manner he assumed, I did not succeed, during the whole interview, in throwing off the uncomfortable feeling his inspection of me caused.

The arguments of the Princess succeeded in convincing the Procureur Impérial that the French empire would not be shaken absolutely to its foundations, by his according us the exemption we had ventured to ask. He need not have granted us this great privilege, but he did so with much show of commiseration for me and my children, and with the very best grace. He promised to communicate with the authorities at the *mairie*, without delay, and he was as good as his word.

Monsieur Questel may or may not have been satisfied we had succeeded, but if he was not really so, he dissimulated. As for the mayor, his surprise admits of no description. It condensed itself into the reiterated and emphatic declaration that he "could not understand it": and for aught I know to the contrary, he may be attempting to this day, to solve the problem.

The way being thus smoothed, and Monsieur Questel having no interest in devising fresh pretexts for deferring the legalization of the marriage, the civil ceremony was celebrated in due form, and the fact inscribed in the municipal records.

I hoped that Ayesha's knowledge of her husband's duplicity, his avowed purpose of betraying her into the hands of her enemies—her father and her mother-in-law—and her experience of his brutal character, would cause her to hesitate to give him the procuration he had been so urgent to obtain. At any rate, I trusted she would abide by my warning not to sign any paper he might present to her for signature, without first consulting me, so that we might have an opportunity of considering its contents. I renewed this caution at the first opportunity, only to learn that she had yielded to his importunities, supported by dark threats, and given him her signature without making herself acquainted with the purport of the document.

CHAPTER XIV.

Monsieur Questel's vacillation—I am sent to Vienna—I return to Paris and am sent to Rome—Interview with Fuad Pasha—Departure for Paris.

PENDING the proceedings narrated in the last chapter, Monsieur Questel made frequent visits to the Ottoman Legation, and once more began to hint at a journey to Constantinople. This did not astonish me, for I had never held any other conviction than that he was manœuvring with the steady purpose in view of getting there with Ayesha. I was, however, in no fear now of his succeeding in that part of his design which related to her, and therefore awaited with confidence his next decisive move. His excuse for going so often to the Legation was to obtain the regularization of his papers. Judging now, after the event, I do not doubt but that he encountered unexpected obstacles which caused him to hesitate, for he had proved he was not the man to advance a single step without making pretty sure of his ground, nor to stop short, without good reasons, in the execution of an enterprise upon which he had set his mind.

It did not, therefore, surprise me when Monsieur Questel informed us, one morning, that he did not now intend to go to Constantinople, but proposed instead that I should set out **for Vienna to see Haida Effendi, the Turkish** Ambassador there. My son-in-law **pretended** he had received intelligence **from** Constantinople which led him to **believe that a** little pressure would produce a satisfactory result. He and Ayesha would return into Brittany and await there the issue of this step.

Haida Effendi was an old friend of mine, and having thoroughly considered the position, **I** determined to comply with Questel's suggestion. I communicated my decision to him, and he handed me a hundred and fifty francs, promising me a remittance by banker's order as soon as I reached **Vienna.**

I remained **fifteen days in** the Austrian capital without receiving a line from my son-in-law. **In** the interval I had several interviews with the Turkish Ambassador, but he said my course in quitting Constantinople had so irritated my husband and his relatives, that it was utterly useless for me to hope for any help from that quarter, and that the marriage of **Ayesha** had added fuel to the fire.

This result of an effort in which I had never much confidence, did not surprise me, and only the want of the requisite funds hindered me from returning to Paris after my first interview with my old friend. Finding that no remittances arrived, nor any communication whatever from Questel, I was compelled to lay my position bare to Haida Effendi, who kindly, for former friendship's sake, gave me five hundred francs. I was thus relieved from my dilemma. I paid my hotel bill and at once returned to Paris, hoping to find a letter of explanation awaiting me there.

I immediately sent a note to my son-in-law, informing him of my return, and asking him what I should do. To this no reply came until three weeks had elapsed, during which period anxiety on the score of my daughter drove me to the very verge of despair. But for my friend Madame Davidoff I must have been reduced to the greatest straits. At her invitation I occupied a room in her apartments, and she most kindly desired me to continue to do so, when—at the expiration of ten days—she left Paris for Italy. Through her, also,

I was introduced to a lady's boarding-house in our neighbourhood, the inmates of which invited me to dine with them daily. In my destitute condition, this act of kindness laid me under deep obligation to my new friends, and to the present day I think of it with gratitude.

At last a letter came from Questel. Ayesha was quite well, a piece of news which greatly relieved my mind. He excused himself for not having sent me money to Vienna, upon the pretext that he believed Haida Effendi, being so old a friend of mine, would be certain to supply me with funds. I need scarcely observe that I felt this to be a mere subterfuge. It was, indeed, one too transparent for me to be deceived by it. Questel went on to say he had heard Fuad Pasha was now in Rome, and I must go thither to make interest with him. I did not see the utility of this course, and my recent Vienna experience satisfied me such a journey would be useless. My friends, the ladies of the boarding-house, rose literally in arms against the suggestion, and the state of my health at that moment further indisposed me to take so long a journey. I wrote to Questel stating my objections, and my own views on the inutility of such a step, but with his reply came a letter from Ayesha beseeching me to go, and to try one last time what I could do. In spite of my own misgivings, of the ladies' warnings, of the indifferent state of my health, I made up my mind to try Fuad Pasha; so I started for Rome with my son-in-law's promise to forward funds to me, and with a hundred and fifty francs which he had sent me for travelling expenses.

On reaching Genoa my passport was demanded, and as I was not provided with this absurd document, my further progress was arrested.

Perhaps no more striking illustration of the inutility of the passport-system, as a police regulation, could be furnished than my own case in the present instance exhibits. As a rule—and this fact the police authorities themselves admit—the parties who have the strongest reasons for evading a too close personal scrutiny, are just those who contrive to be invariably and scrupulously *en règle*; and these same authorities will acknowledge that only for "other means" of detection at their disposal, suspected individuals and others who are "wanted," would escape. Such facts suggest the inquiry why these "other means" are not made use of to the benefit of the genuine traveller; and why—to carry out a system admitted to be inoperative—the latter must be subjected to the annoyances, delays, and other minor nuisances, which the non-possession of that acknowledged useless and absurd document, a passport, entails.

In my dilemma, I had but the one resource of applying to the Turkish Consul, an Armenian. In answer to his questions I was compelled to draw rather largely and boldly upon my imagination for my nationality and parentage. Upon his requesting my name, I gave him one I knew to be Armenian, but which certainly was not mine. Next, he asked me for my father's, a query that brought me to a sudden stand-still; then I hesitated, and said I did not know, at which he laughed rather heartily, commenting upon the extraordinary fact of my ignorance on so important a point. I excused myself by pleading confusion of ideas arising from over-fatigue, but another Armenian name occurring to me at the moment, I gave it. He looked fixedly at me, and told me I did not look like an Armenian, and, in fact, that he believed me to be some princess in disguise. He proceeded, nevertheless, to make out my passport, which he very reverently handed to me; and upon my intimating—in answer to a recommendation from him not to proceed further on my journey that day—that the state of my finances rendered any delay on the road impossible, he begged my acceptance of a hundred francs, and insisted upon his servant's accompanying me to the steam-packet office, where I wished to take my place for the next departure.

I got off next morning early, by the steamer to Civita Vecchia, and on my arrival in Rome found that my sole fortune amounted to the hundred francs which the Consul had presented me with. An omnibus, waiting for passengers, took me in, in a two-fold sense. I told the driver I did not wish to go to an expensive hotel, and asked if his vehicle —in which were some English ladies—belonged to one of this class. He laughed, and looked at me as though he were astonished I could think him capable of conveying passengers to any but the cheapest hotel. He went further, and assured me the one he would take me to was the best and cheapest in Rome. If dearest is in the end cheapest, he may have been right; and if I had only reflected for a single moment, I might have felt satisfied, from the fact of his omnibus containing English ladies, that a cheap hotel was the very last he would convey them to. It was midnight when we reached it, and for the benefit of travellers who may not like to frequent a cheap hotel, I will add that the one in question was the Hotel de Rome, and that my entertainment for that one night—my supper-dinner, and my breakfast next morning included—was charged me only sixty francs ; though how the bill was made out, has remained for me an insolvable arithmetical problem. I admit the magnificence of the apartments, the sumptuousness of the refections, and the minute attentions of the waiters, but sixty francs is, decidedly, not—cheap, for one night.

It was by way of precaution I asked for my bill in the morning, the painful consciousness of a low exchequer prompting me to the act : not rash under such circumstances, but highly prudent. I immediately started off to hunt for a private lodging, and having fortunately discovered one, after a not too long search, during which I had no unfavourable opportunity of taking stock of the accumulated filth of the city of the Seven Hills, I returned to the hotel, discharged my account like one of the ancient princesses—fabulous personages who are reputed never to have checked even their dress-makers' bills—and departed to my new quarters.

My sole object in coming to Rome was to see Fuad Pasha ; and being ignorant of his abode, I questioned the porter of the hotel with a view to ascertain whether he knew his Excellency's address. The worthy porter—who from his habit of answering questions was always on the look-out for them, and wore the air of a perpetual note of interrogation—informed me that his Imperial Excellency had done them—himself and his employers—the distinguished honour of occupying a suite in their hotel, and that if Madame—myself—desired an interview with his Imperial Excellency, the mode of approaching his august person was to see his physician, who also officiated as his Chamberlain. I declined the immediate honour, but made the grandiose porter my friend by a present of two francs.

After my tedious and fatiguing journey I was glad to take a little rest, and accordingly kept to my apartment for a couple of days. I then repaired to the Hotel de Rome, and upon sending in my card, was ushered into the presence of the regulator of Fuad Pasha's health. His Mightiness condescended to inquire the nature of my business with his master. My name had, I am sure, given him a sufficiently strong suspicion of my errand, to furnish him with a cue for his course. His Excellency was not in robust health; had over-much to attend to; required one day's previous notice of a visit; could not be seen then, but perhaps would receive me **next** day. But whilst he was thus occupied in framing excuses for not presenting me, **a card** was brought in, and was followed **by** a priest, whom his Excellency—apologising for quitting me—at once introduced into **an inner** room, where I felt sure the Pasha was at that moment. **When he returned** he found **me gone.**

This physician was an Armenian, whose countenance **inspired me with** mistrust. I resolved not to allow him to be intermediary between me and the Pasha on the occasion of my second visit. I had a note ready for Fuad himself, and my friend the porter having informed me the Armenian was not lying-in-wait, I sent in the note, **and was at** once admitted.

Fuad Pasha was really **ill: ill of the malady** which **ultimately, and not so long after, carried** him off. He was, **at this** moment, travelling for his health. He received me cordially, and expressed **his regret to see me in such a sad** position. He said it **was my** own fault; I ought never **to** have quitted **Constantinople.**

I reminded him **that I had not done so** until compelled—had, in fact, been driven to it by persecutions in which he had himself participated—and that I **had done** nothing **to** bring down upon me such a penalty as then threatened me. My daughter had sought refuge with me, and my duty, as a mother, was to cherish and protect her.

Fuad Pasha then referred to the imperious, impetuous, and implacable character of my husband, dwelling upon certain violent scenes in the Council, and of his disrespect—when excited—even of the Sultan, as proofs of his obduracy to reason, and as showing how unlikely he was to be influenced by considerations of any kind in a case in which his pride had been outraged, and his authority set at nought. He said our flight into Europe had been a great scandal, and that the baptism of Ayesha into the Catholic Church, then her marriage with one of an Infidel race, had exasperated Kibrizli to the last degree, and also greatly incensed the Turks, who considered we had brought a disgrace upon them. Nevertheless, he thought, if we returned to Constantinople, matters might be arranged, and go on more smoothly; but so long as we remained in Europe, nothing would be done for us.

Our interview lasted for upwards of an hour. He could not assist me much, he said, for he did not like to ask his Chamberlain for money, but he handed me ten napoleons, all he had about him, and I took my leave quite satisfied there was no hope of justice from Constantinople.

During my stay at Rome, which lasted two weeks, I saw Fuad Pasha only that once. At the expiration of this period, finding that no letter arrived for me from home, and that my funds were reduced to fifty francs, I decided to return to Paris. I did not even stay to pay my respects to the Pope, although Monsignor Talbot came to see me, in consequence of a letter he had received from Madame Davidoff, and would have presented me to His Holiness.

CHAPTER XV.

My journey to Geneva—Misadventures by the way—Monseigneur de Marseilles and Sister Josephine of the Convent of La Grande Miséricorde.

I RETURNED to Genoa by way of Florence, and on my arrival at the former city, called upon my friend the Consul—the Armenian—but he had gone to the place I had just left. Without delay I took passage for Nice on board a small steamer. The weather was miserable; rain in torrents, high wind, and a heavy sea. I am not favoured by Neptune; and when upon the element which he rules so irregularly, own to but one desire, namely, to tread firm ground again as soon as possible. There were very many other passengers; but under the circumstances we were anything but a pleasant company.

I was between two spells of the aggravating malady with which the majority of travellers by sea are familiar, and had reached that condition of doziness and inertia it engenders, when to be disturbed is the last degree of mortal misery. All at once loud shouts, accompanied with rapid and heavy tramping of hurried feet, roused me and my fellow-sufferers from our state of torpor, and presently the vessel began to roll heavily from side to side. We no longer heard the flapping of her paddle-wheels, nor the thud-thud of her engines, nor felt the uncomfortable tremor through her frame indicating resistance to the power which was driving her forward. The more convalescent amongst the company looked up with an air of alarmed inquisitiveness; the worst did not stir, satisfied that nothing more unendurable could be their fate, than that the vessel should continue her uneasy course; the others uttered exclamations of alarm, and shouted for the steward to inform them what had happened. After a considerable lapse of time he appeared. He said "it was only the engines which had broken down," and that instead of continuing our journey to Nice we should be compelled to disembark at Port Ferrati, near Vintimille. This we did, at three o'clock in the morning, in a continuous down-pour of rain, in the dark, and most of us more dead than alive.

I think if any one had whispered in my ear that I was about to be consigned to the bottom of the sea, I should have been content to accept my fate. How I reached the shore I am utterly unable to say. I retain a hazy recollection of gaining the deck by a pre-concerted arrangement on the part of those who executed me, and that it was effected by a complicated movement during which my sensations were of being shouldered, and hoisted, and dragged and borne along, a helpless inert mass; of being pitched into a boat, and almost immediately afterwards of being nearly pitched out of it again; of another terrible turn of plunging, and rolling, and tossing, then of a renewal of the process of locomotion, with an irrepressible desire to stop the world from turning round; lastly, of a consciousness that I was not at the Antipodes of Paradise, but in a carriage of some sort, and that I had lost my luggage, namely, two bags, containing my remnant of ready cash, my papers, and sundry necessary articles of wearing apparel.

I was indebted to a fellow-passenger, a lady, for the charity of a place of rest for a few hours, and for refreshment as soon as I could take it. She also was going to Nice, and offered to take me with her. I accepted her proposal with alacrity and gratitude. We started that same day, for in my predicament I could not stay to make inquiries about my lost luggage; an office which the landlord of the hotel undertook, but without result. My kind companion conducted me to her hotel, and we parted next day, she continuing her journey.

Without money, luggage, or friends, I had no time to lose. I went straightway to the Turkish Consul—Count Constantin—to whom I related my story and my latest misadventure. He was a fine old man, and dwelt in a grand house, in the midst of a beautiful garden, planted with groves of orange trees, and having a fountain in the centre of the flower-patch. He invited me to dinner, and was most kind and courteous. He told me, however, he had received the strictest orders not to assist any Turks; out of consideration for my position, nevertheless, he gave me sufficient to pay my way, and to get to Marseilles.

I had another purpose in view in going to Marseilles. I had a niece in Lyons—the daughter of my sister—who was married to a wealthy silk manufacturer. He supplied the Sultan and his household with gold brocaded silks and other rich stuffs, and I felt sure an appeal to her would be successful.

But how was I to get to Lyons without money?

There was the Turkish Consul, of course, and

my first visit was to him. He was an old Frenchman, and possessed all the national characteristics of excessive politeness. I laid bare my position, and asked him for money to help me forward. He expressed his intense regret, his desolation at being compelled to refuse assistance to a lady in such a pitiable case, but his orders were not to give money-help to promiscuous travellers in France, and to such Turkish subjects only as were returning to Constantinople. I could not make the slightest impression upon him, so we parted, probably with mutual unfavourable opinions of each other.

I had about me a letter given to me at my request by the Abbé Boré, setting forth my name and quality, and recommending me and my daughter. It was, in fact, a certificate of identity. I had obtained it in the earlier days of our acquaintance, by way of precaution, to serve a special purpose in case of need. Aware of the Abbé's popularity in all the religious establishments in France, I bethought me of making use of my letter to procure an introduction to the Superior of one of these in Marseilles. Accordingly, I presented myself to the Directress of the Convent of the Sisters of Charity of St. Vincent de Paul; told her, in brief, my history; exposed my position, and solicited help.

The worthy lady listened to my narrative, expressed her regret that she could not assist me, then, with exquisite politeness, recommended me to **apply to** the Lady Superior of the Convent of La Grande Miséricorde. Subduing by an effort my extreme disappointment at such a reception, I quitted **this** grand Sister **of Charity with a heavy heart, and** made **my way to the Convent of Great Mercy. Here my reception was still** less encouraging. I had to send **in my** name, then **to** explain the nature of my errand; next, to wait until the Lady Superior had taken her time to consider my application; and, finally, to endure the mortification of receiving a curt message that she **could not give** me anything. Thus rebuffed, **I returned to my hotel** deeply pained and **discouraged.**

I then thought of the Bishop, **and, notwith**standing **he bore the character of being** extremely avaricious, **I proceeded to his** residence, **having** easily **ascertained his address.** I was received **by** a valet, who **declined to** disturb Monseigneur unless I communicated **my business.** As **to do this** did not suit **my purpose,** and as I saw **that the** valet was inflexible,—whether acting upon **orders** or otherwise—I once more returned **to** my hotel, having matured a little plot by which I hoped to

P

obtain access to Monseigneur without being filtered through his man-servant.

I re-adjusted my dress, and borrowed from the landlady—to whom I confided my secret—a handsome shawl, which I arranged after the Oriental style, so as to partially conceal my face, and, thus attired, once more sallied forth.

My friend the valet did not recognise me. I handed him my card, upon which was written "Madame la Princesse Kibrizli," and intimated that I had something to give to Monseigneur. In a very few minutes I was invited to walk up-stairs, on the landing of which Monseigneur, in full canonical robes, stood ready to receive me.

Monseigneur de Marseilles was a man of imposing appearance, but although his countenance wore a certain air of benevolence, a closer scrutiny betrayed an inner man out of harmony with his vocation. Nevertheless I really expected to find him ready to help the needy, of which class I felt myself to be, just then, the neediest representative. He was all smiles and suavity. He was probably accustomed to receive gifts for charitable purposes from the hands of grand ladies, and, no doubt, imagined I was one come for some such purpose. I handed him the Abbé Boré's letter, and became almost frightened at the change it wrought in his countenance. Whether he fancied I had imposed upon him in obtaining access to his gracious presence by an unworthy device, or whether the Abbé's recommendation of us as worthy of receiving help in a case of emergency touched the weakest of his weak points, I will not venture to say: but he became a transformed man. His forehead corrugated into wrinkles; his nose worked and twisted about in a most extraordinary manner; his lips trembled, and his whole frame became convulsed. I feared, seeing him thus moved, he was going into a fit. He muttered some incoherent sentences relating to the object of my visit, to the numerous claims upon him, and so forth: in the meantime writing a hurried note, which he hastened to place in my hand, telling me it was to be taken to Sister Josephine, the Lady Superior of the Convent of the Grande Miséricorde. Of course, I did not inform him I had already troubled Sister Josephine. I accepted his letter to her, with an expression of thanks, hoping it would have the effect of opening her heart, and satisfied that, at any rate, it would ensure me a more courteous reception.

On reaching the convent, I informed the Sister in attendance that I had a message from the Bishop to the Lady Superior, whom I must see. She conveyed this intimation to Sister Josephine, and soon returned with a request that I would follow her. She conducted me into a fine, large, well-appointed saloon, in which the Lady Superior occupied a comfortable arm-chair. She arose, and advanced to meet me, took me by both hands, and led me to a chair by the side of her own. Evidently my coming quite fresh from the Bishop gave me a degree of importance in her eyes I could not pretend to on my own individual merits: surrounded me, in fact, with an atmosphere of sanctity which, though second-hand, it was agreeable to her to imbibe. She was wholly wrapt up in him. Monseigneur was in every sentence she uttered. I was delighted, for I augured favourably for myself from her veneration for him. I did not know the contents of his letter to her. She received it from my hands with a daintiness I could not but remark; with a touch-me-not sort of air, no doubt in harmony with the reverential sentiments she professed for so saintly a man.

I am unable to suggest what she thought the letter contained. Its purport was manifestly not agreeable, judging from the changing expression of her countenance, which I watched narrowly.

Having read the note, she got up solemnly, went to a drawer in her writing-table, out of which she took some money, and, returning, said she felt great pleasure in complying with Monseigneur's request. With this, she placed in my hand, with a stately air, the sum of THREE FRANCS.

Sister Josephine seemed more embarrassed in giving me this benefaction than I was to receive it. I felt humiliated to the very ground, but I was also indignant; and as soon as I had recovered from my first surprise, gave utterance to my feelings without reserve, and in plain, honest language. Sister Josephine made no reply to my severe strictures upon the meanness of the Bishop's procedure, and on her own lack of feeling, further than an observation to the effect that she had no control over Monseigneur's charities, and was not herself in a position to supply the wants of such persons as myself. For my own part, I was in none to refuse a gift, how small soever. I told her so, and that I therefore accepted hers, but that I sincerely pitied those persons whose necessities drove them to lay her charity under contribution, and so quitted her.

Finding that to expect help from the conventual sisterhoods of the city was a hopeless resource, no alternative remained to me but to dispose of a portion of my wearing apparel; for I had a week's hotel-account to discharge, as well as the cost of my journey to Lyons to provide for. I therefore sold a cloth cloak and a ring, and having paid my bill and obtained my ticket, found myself left with a single franc.

CHAPTER XVI.

My first night in Lyons—My wanderings in search of a shelter—The Hospital for the Destitute—My fellow-patients—Night scene in my Ward—Succour from Paris.

On arriving at Lyons, I lost no time in hunting up my niece. The nature of her husband's business suggested to me the kind of shops to resort to for the information I required. After some little wandering about, I ascertained he had given up business and gone with his wife to Constantinople some three months before my arrival, in consequence of the decease of her father, whose heiress she was. This news was a grievous disappointment of my hopes.

My next experiment was to find an hotel, but as I presented myself without baggage, payment in advance was demanded of me. This I was unprepared to make; and after many applications of this kind, I gave up the attempt.

Thoroughly disheartened, footsore, weary, and hungry, and without a shelter, I was in a more pitiable plight than the veriest wretch in the city. I wandered through the ill-paved streets, seeking a rest but finding none, and a prey to the bitterest anguish of mind. At last, in a bye-street, I met an old woman, whose sharp, inquisitive glance at me as I passed induced me to speak to her. I told her I was a tired traveller; that relations whom I expected to find in the city had quitted it; that I had failed to get an hotel, as I was without baggage; and that I was seeking a place of accommodation for the night. I wound up by asking whether she could recommend me to anyone for a lodging. She answered by offering to let me sleep at her own place, if I would go to it. I assented at once, and she straightway conducted me to her home.

It was a very humble abode, and not over tidy, for she had but the one room for all purposes. In a recess in it stood a good and a clean bed. This she considerately gave up to me, making shift herself upon a mattress laid on the floor. I was so worn-out with fatigue that I felt glad to lie down, though I had not eaten a morsel that day. Nature asserted her claims, nevertheless, and the fumes arising from a certain earthenware pot, standing in the hot embers of a wood fire, tantalized me severely with their savoury odour. I did not like to tell my hostess I was hungry, and fortunately her hospitality spared me from this humiliation, for she presently said that perhaps I might like to partake of her *pot-au-feu*. I need scarcely add I was only too glad to do so, and right welcome and delicious was that by no means plenteous meal after so prolonged a fast.

Ten o'clock had struck next morning before I awoke, and I felt quite revived by my long sleep. It was mortifying to me in the extreme to have to confess to my hostess, when she claimed two francs as the price of my entertainment, that I did not possess the amount. I gave her my last franc, and told her I was going to write to my friends in Paris for a remittance, and would pay her handsomely as soon as it came to hand. She replied that she could not afford to provide for me, and unless I paid her the two francs I must seek shelter and food elsewhere. I could not blame the woman for this plain dealing, though the consequences to me threatened to be serious. I was an utter stranger to her; knew no one in Lyons to whom I could refer; had no luggage, and therefore had not any right to expect a poor woman to take charge of me upon my bare word that I would pay her at some indeterminate period. But what was I to do now?

The old lady told me there were several convents in Lyons where the Sisters gave help to necessitous persons, and that probably I should obtain, at one or other of these, the assistance I needed. The prospect was not cheering, nor did I consider it encouraging, with my too recent experiences of conventual benevolence still fresh in my memory. But no other resource was open to me. I took the address of my hostess, and leaving instructions with her to receive any letter coming for me, I once more set out upon my wanderings.

To find a public writer was my first errand. I was not long in discovering one, at the corner of a street, sitting in his place of business, or *bureau*; an enlarged sentry-box with windows on three sides of it, upon which sundry specimens of caligraphy were stuck with wafers, and which did duty for advertisements of his calling. I explained to him my need of his services, and the kind of letter I desired him to write. My appeal was to my friends at the ladies' boarding-house, Rue du Bac, Paris, to whom it was absolutely necessary I should state how I was then circumstanced. I found the writer did business upon the ready-money principle only, for he at once intimated that he should require **payment before** he put **pen to paper.** As no promise of mine to pay him **upon** receipt of the remittance I felt sure would come in a few days, produced the slightest effect, no alternative remained to me **but to try in** some other quarter.

After a few turns, I entered the shop of a silk-mercer, **the assistant in** which not only wrote my letter, but put a stamp upon it: a small favour this, yet one so kindly and considerately conferred as to give it a certain magnitude in my estimation it is gratifying to me to record.

It now became imperative **to** seek an asylum, and means of obtaining food, **until** the answer to my letter should arrive. I roamed through the streets in search of the convents at which **I had** been led to expect I should find **what I sought,** but disappointment waited persistently **upon me.** At one of these establishments the Sister gave me **two** tickets—one for bread, **the** other for meat—to be **presented at another place.** I had to inquire **my** way, and **found I should have to** walk to quite the remotest suburb **of the city.** It would have taken me two hours to **reach the spot, and** feeling myself unequal to so formidable a task, **I** returned to the convent and gave back the tickets to the Sister, explaining why **I** could not make use of them.

She merely said she was sorry, and dismissed me complacently once more into the street.

It was now near evening. I had not broken my fast that day. I was sinking from exhaustion, as well as from excessive fatigue. I must, by this time, have visited almost every quarter of the city, and being quite at the end of my devices, I had made up my mind to return to my hostess of the previous night and make an appeal to her womanly feelings. With this object in view, I set out in the direction of her dwelling, inquiring my way as I proceeded. A sudden turn brought me into a large street I did not recognise, in which stood a structure of immense extent. It turned out to be an Hospital for the Destitute. My poor heart bounded. Here, at any rate, I thought, I shall find a temporary refuge. Nevertheless, I durst not at first enter the place. I passed the door two or three times before I could decide to go in, but, finally, plucking up courage, entered, and asked to see the doctor.

I was conducted into the presence of the second physician, who, after feeling my pulse, gave me a note to hand to the Lady Superior. He put no questions to me, no doubt because he at once perceived that mine was only a case of debility; but

I told him I came from Turkey, and as I afterwards became known by the name of "La Turque," I conclude he so described me. I found the Lady Superior in a saloon up-stairs, and though I was really ill of fatigue, I could not help laughing when, after reading the paper, she looked over it at me, and asked where the sick person was. I introduced myself, then, in this capacity—feeling somewhat ashamed of my own lustiness—whereupon she called a sister-attendant, and I was taken up into a ward, where lay some sixty or more patients, most of them suffering from lung complaints. I was given over to the care of one of the attendants, who at once proceeded to undress me; and my clothes having been put up into a bundle, I went to bed.

In the course of an hour or so I was aroused from a doze by the clatter of knives and forks and the odour of savoury food. The sensations thus provoked I may leave to the imagination of all who have, either from necessity or from accident, fasted for an inordinate time. I had arrived too late for the day-meal, but the prospect of supper kept under control my impatience for food, though it in no wise allayed my craving for it. Greedily, I may honestly confess, did I watch the distribution of the rations to the other patients until all were served. Yet no portion came to me. I then called to the sister-attendant, who—to my intense surprise and grievous disappointment—informed me that the rules of the establishment prohibited the giving of food to any patient until the doctor had judged of the nature of the case and issued instructions accordingly. In vain I appealed to the sister. She answered me kindly, but turned an inexorably deaf ear to my entreaties, and I was obliged to compose myself to doze again, and to appease the wolf within, with promises to satisfy his demands on the morrow.

But sleep was now impossible. This was my first experience as an inmate of an hospital, and my attention became concentrated upon my companions.

No spectacle could possibly be more depressing than that presented by so many wan, haggard faces: so many sunken, gleaming eyes: so many prostrate forms, quiescent, corpse-like under their white coverlets. As I sat and gazed at them, there were moments when I fancied myself an inhabitant of some chamber of the dead, awaiting the resurrection and the judgment. Then would come full consciousness of the reality, vividly brought home to me by the manifestations of suffering I was compelled to witness. It was terrible to have to listen to the painful breathing, the moans, the distressed coughing of so many fellow-creatures, many of them in the last stages of consumption ; and nothing but the pressure of the direst necessity reconciled me to endure the sight of such an amount of human misery. Such a night I had never passed in my life, and what I witnessed will remain indelibly impressed upon my memory.

I cannot say I once slept through the long, weary hours of that never-ending night. If I lost consciousness for the briefest period, it was only to be again startled into wakefulness by the moans of some sufferer, impatient of pain, and by a renewal of the distressing emotions which, in my position, such sounds and such a scene were calculated to engender. But morning came at last, with all the quiet bustle incidental to the preparation of the ward for the doctors' inspection of the patients.

It did not take mine long to sum up my case. He felt my pulse, asked me sundry questions, such as whence I came, whither I was travelling, how long I had been in the city, what I had been doing, where I had lodged the previous night, and so forth ; and having written something upon a card—which was afterwards hung at the foot of my bed—he patted me encouragingly upon the shoulder, told me he thought he quite understood my malady, and calling the sister-attendant, bade her provide me with the best herb-drinks, and to give me two full rations of food: these to be continued every day.

I fancied his intelligent, benevolent countenance beamed with a humorous smile as—after giving his instructions—he again turned to me, to add the expression of a hope that in a few days I might be sufficiently well to make room for another patient. I responded by an assurance of the fullest confidence in his treatment, and of my desire not to remain in the hospital one hour longer than the time requisite for the re-establishment of my strength.

The kind doctor's instructions—I cannot style them prescriptions—were faithfully observed by the equally kind sisters, and I soon began to experience the benefit of them. Indeed the greatest attention was paid, not only to me, but to all the patients. The soups and the more material food were of the best quality, and the full rations most abundant. The hospital is one of the largest in France, is richly endowed, and deserves all the support and patronage it commands. I have the best reasons for expressing my gratitude for the treatment I experienced in it.

I have said that the beds were occupied chiefly by consumptive patients, or by such as were suffering from lung complaints. Those right and left of me were of this class. One of these invalids was of advanced age, and coughed incessantly: I ought rather to say, barked. The other was quite young. The elder invalid bored and tormented the doctor and the sisters with questions respecting the chances of her recovery, her own speculations being affirmative. I believe her malady was asthma. The young girl—who was evidently fast taking leave of life—bore her sufferings meekly and resignedly, and often did not stir for hours. The old lady not only coughed, but groaned piteously between whiles, to the disturbance and inconvenience of everybody in her vicinity. When remonstrated with by the sister, she would answer: "What will you? it relieves me!" I was uncharitable enough to wish the effect were less salutary; for, between her groans and her coughing-fits, sleep was most difficult, and not refreshing.

In the middle of the second night a priest was called in to administer the last rites of the Church to a dying inmate of our ward. In the deep gloom —scarcely relieved by the dull glimmer of a few night-lights—priest and sister-attendants, in their habiliments of black and white, looked like so many shades gliding about. In the semi-darkness they clustered, in a kneeling posture, around the bed of the moribund, and so remained until the *viaticum* and the last blessing had solaced her dying moments. The young patient at my side—although she had not moved for some time—turned her large, lustrous eyes towards this lugubrious scene, and, making a considerable effort, sat up. Presently she withdrew from beneath her pillow a chaplet, and bowing her head reverently, as the low muttering of the priest's voice reached her ears, whispered her prayers whilst telling off her beads, one by one, with her worn, transparent fingers. As the solemn group at the lower end began to disperse, she sank back, quite exhausted, breathing in a succession of little pants, her large eyes still open and fixed upon the figure of the priest vanishing in the obscurity. Soon the sister-attendant was at her bedside.

"Dost thou feel any better, my child?" she asked, as she adjusted the pillow and smoothed down the coverlet.

"I hope to do—soon!" the young girl replied, in a scarcely audible whisper: "Soon— soon!"

"Let us hope so too, then," responded the sister;

but, as our eyes met, I saw that she hoped without faith.

I had passed three nights in the establishment, and such rest as I had been able to obtain and abundance of good food had quite restored me. On the morning of the third day, the doctor asked me if I felt sufficiently well to leave; adding, that, in such case, and if I were in any trouble, he would see how far he could assist me. I thanked him gratefully, and told him I was hourly expecting news from my friends in Paris; but, should I be disappointed, I would seek his advice and aid.

I had already made up my mind to go out, for I felt reluctant to impose upon the generosity of the administration, and I knew the time had more than elapsed for a letter to arrive for me by return post from Paris. I intended going at once to ascertain whether my hostess of the first night had received one; for she did not know where I was, as I had no fixed destination when I quitted her. All at once, and immensely to my amazement, I saw her enter the ward. She soon perceived me, and immediately held up her hand, waving in it, over her head, a letter. A few minutes brought her to my bed-side, and placed me in possession of the contents of the missive.

It was a hundred francs Bank of France note.

The old lady had taken considerable trouble to discover me by going the round of the charitable establishments which were likely to have assisted me. I was not long in dressing myself, and we went out together. Whilst she obtained change, I got a few lines of thanks written and addressed to the doctor of the asylum, and transmitted to him through the porter. The old lady would now gladly enough have received me. I did not care to satisfy myself of the sincerity of her delight at witnessing my own, nor to accept her urgent offers of service. I was impatient to get to Paris without delay, and, having given her ten francs, lost no time in getting to the railway station, where we parted.

CHAPTER XVII.

My return to Paris—My daughter's arrival—Monsieur Questel's excuses—A new personage appears on the scene—We leave for Messina with Monsieur Questel—His change of plan—He tries to lure us to Constantinople, and, as we will not go, he proceeds thither himself—The issue, and the last of M. Questel.

To thank my friends of the ladies' boarding-house was my first care; and delighted they were to see me again, though they did not fail to unite in a grand chorus of "We told you how it would be." The invitation to take my daily meals with them was renewed and joyfully accepted. They could not offer me lodging accommodation, so I had to seek that in an adjoining hotel. I was, however, fortunate enough, within a few days, to meet with a lady, an old friend of mine, who kindly offered me an apartment until my affairs should take a favourable turn, or I should hear from my daughter, whose apparent indifference and neglect of me were severely commented upon by everybody who knew us.

I remained two months in a state of terrible anguish, for I could obtain no reply to my repeated communications. During this time of suspense, the ladies were most kind to me. Now, came a present of clothing; then, a gift in money. They did not leave me in want of anything. One gave me a gold watch; others begged my acceptance of trinkets. Never was petted child more spoiled. I am sure no spoiled and petted child was ever half so grateful.

One forenoon—at the end of this period—being in the midst of my friends, I was startled by the sound of Ayesha's voice. The door was suddenly thrown open, and she came bounding in, followed by her husband. In the joy of that meeting with her, all my late troubles, fatigues, disappointments, anxieties, were forgotten. She referred me to Questel for explanations, and he was at no loss for excuses. His chief reason for silence was the delay, from day to day, in the settlement of his affairs. He had been treating for the sale of his property in Brittany, his intention being to purchase some land at Messina, and settle down there. He had hoped for the conclusion of this business more than two months ago, and, as he wished me to accompany him and Ayesha, he had deferred communicating with me until matters were definitively settled.

I frankly admit I did not wholly believe my son-in-law's story, though I gave him no reason to suppose this to be the fact. I strongly suspected him of having in view a remoter destination which he would probably devise means of preventing me from reaching. Ayesha, I found, had consented to go, only upon the condition of my accompanying her: a proposition he had at first combated, and, finally, had not agreed to, until Ayesha had told him resolutely, she would not stir without me. This information decided me. My friends, the ladies of the boarding-house, endeavoured in vain to dissuade me from my purpose, threatening never to speak to me again. My daughter, they said, was quite old enough to take care of herself; and if she preferred going away with her husband, I was not justified in making myself a slave to her wishes and caprices. I should only be treated with unkindness and ingratitude by herself and her husband; in fact, they urged arguments of which I felt the full force, but which were impotent against maternal love and sense of duty. None of them were mothers, and therefore none could enter into my feelings and fears. I could only dwell upon these as excuses for what they called my weakness, and represent that she was my only comfort, and that I manche's Bank of General Credit, Monsieur Questel expressed a wish to learn something more about it, as he desired to put his capital out at interest. I therefore took him to the office of Monsieur Decourdemanche for further information, though nothing came of the interview so far as I know. I mention the incident because this visit brought me once more into personal communication with Monsieur Decourdemanche, whose acquaintance—as will be found—has seriously affected my life ever since, and in the most sinister manner.

Not many days after, he called upon me with an invitation to meet at dinner the friends of whom he had spoken, and who were to assemble in the apartments of a Monsieur Paton, in the Rue de la Madeleine. I did not then know that this gentleman wrote upon Turkish affairs, under an anonymous name, in the *Gaulois* newspaper, nor that a Monsieur Leblond, another of the party, a barrister, was upon intimate terms with Djemil Pasha, the Turkish Ambassador in Paris. Had I been aware of these facts, I should certainly not have trusted myself in such suspicious company. In my ignorance I accepted the proffered invitation.

The dinner was choice in all its appointments, and extreme courtesy was shown to me. The conversation, confined to Turkey and its affairs, was left principally to me; probably, as I afterwards suspected, with an ulterior object. If, however, the Turkish Ambassador's spy lay in wait to catch me, he was welcome to the truths he heard, and to report them to his patron.

The reader must not imagine I am seeking to raise myself into importance by suggesting, without good reasons, that what I might say of Turkey and its policy had an interest for the representatives of that country. The Turkish Government is exceedingly sensitive to public opinion, and morbidly jealous of its reputation : such as it is. It cannot bear that the truth should be told of its internal corruption, of its demoralizing institutions, of its degrading domestic customs, habits, manners. Least of all can it endure that its foreign policy should be laid bare, and the reasons which govern it. As a rule, no individual really capable of furnishng reliable information to Europeans quits Turkey without being subjected to systematic espionage, with a view to counteract the effect his revelations —if unfavourable—may produce. No European, however acute, can acquire in Turkey any but the most superficial knowledge of its internal or its external polity The harem and its mysteries are mauche's Bank of General Credit, Monsieur Questel expressed a wish to learn something more about it, as he desired to put his capital out at interest. I therefore took him to the office of Monsieur Decourdemanche for further information, though nothing came of the interview so far as I know. I mention the incident because this visit brought me once more into personal communication with Monsieur Decourdemanche, whose acquaintance—as will be found—has seriously affected my life ever since, and in the most sinister manner.

Not many days after, he called upon me with an invitation to meet at dinner the friends of whom he had spoken, and who were to assemble in the apartments of a Monsieur Paton, in the Rue de la Madeleine. I did not then know that this gentleman wrote upon Turkish affairs, under an anonymous name, in the *Gaulois* newspaper, nor that a Monsieur Leblond, another of the party, a barrister, was upon intimate terms with Djemil Pasha, the Turkish Ambassador in Paris. Had I been aware of these facts, I should certainly not have trusted myself in such suspicious company. In my ignorance I accepted the proffered invitation.

The dinner was choice in all its appointments, and extreme courtesy was shown to me. The conversation, confined to Turkey and its affairs, was left principally to me; probably, as I afterwards suspected, with an ulterior object. If, however, the Turkish Ambassador's spy lay in wait to catch me, he was welcome to the truths he heard, and to report them to his patron.

The reader must not imagine I am seeking to raise myself into importance by suggesting, without good reasons, that what I might say of Turkey and its policy had an interest for the representatives of that country. The Turkish Government is exceedingly sensitive to public opinion, and morbidly jealous of its reputation: such as it is. It cannot bear that the truth should be told of its internal corruption, of its demoralizing institutions, of its degrading domestic customs, habits, manners. Least of all can it endure that its foreign policy should be laid bare, and the reasons which govern it. As a rule, no individual really capable of furnishng reliable information to Europeans quits Turkey without being subjected to systematic espionage, with a view to counteract the effect his revelations —if unfavourable—may produce. No European, however acute, can acquire in Turkey any but the most superficial knowledge of its internal or its external polity. The harem and its mysteries are closed against him; official lips are sealed in his presence; and ignorance of the language, Turkish reserve, and, I may add, dislike and suspicion of the Giaour shut him out from every avenue of information. Under such circumstances, it may be imagined with what uneasiness and jealousy Turkish subjects are watched, who may take it into their heads to tell the truth and shame the Grand Turk. To their honour, however, be it said, Turks are faithful to their country and to their fellow-countrymen, and do not depreciate either to foreigners; on the contrary, they rather seek to conceal what may expose them to adverse criticism, and to exaggerate whatever may tend to their glory and honour.

I stood in an exceptional position. My experience of Turkish life, in all its phases, was such as had fallen to the lot of no European woman. As a wife, no secrets of the inner domestic circle of Turkish society were unknown to me. As the wife of the first minister of the empire, I knew facts bearing upon and illustrative of the whole system of its policy, home and foreign. I had myself personal knowledge as a ruler; for it was notorious that Melek-Hanum Kibrizli enjoyed the fullest confidence of her husband, and that her counsels guided him in his administration of public affairs. Bearing in mind these facts, the reader will understand why, apart from private reasons, I could not fail to be an object of suspicion to the Turkish authorities, and why they would have special motives for watching me closely, and reporting what I said and did. I have, therefore, no hesitation in avowing my belief that the dinner to which I was invited was no mere compliment to me, but had for its object to draw me into a trap, of which certain Turkish officials held the strings. The sequel will demonstrate how far I am justified in entertaining this conviction.

We had now been about three weeks in Paris, and the preparations for our journey were completed. I noticed, however, as our arrangements advanced, that Questel seemed more and more disinclined to let me accompany him and his wife; but my daughter's entreaties that I should not leave her rendered me obtuse to all his hints, and indifferent to all his manœuvres and excuses for delay. Entirely baffled, and further subterfuges failing, he was compelled to make a decisive move, and, accordingly, he took out our tickets for Marseilles.

I had resolved merely to see Ayesha settled at

Messina, then, to return to Paris in the event of my finding it impossible to remain with her. I had a good stock of clothes, four or five hundred francs in gold, my watch and trinkets, and sundry other small valuables. My money with such articles as might readily be converted into cash, I took with me; but my trunk I left behind, my sole luggage consisting of a travelling-bag containing a few indispensable garments. We were to start for Messina, from Marseilles, by steamer. Upon our arrival at the station, I expected to see Questel busy himself about his luggage. Seeing he made no move, I remarked to Ayesha upon the strangeness of the fact. She then asked him where their baggage was. He replied that it had been sent forward to Messina from Vannes. The explanation struck me as suspicious; yet it was feasible, and might be the reason why Ayesha and Questel were not more burdened with effects than I myself was.

We took the steamer, in due course, for Messina, but during the voyage, Monsieur Questel did not pay us the smallest attention. I overheard him several times making game of us to the passengers. He also told them he intended to take his wife back to her father, as he had no inclination to remain burdened with her. When he addressed us it was in terms of insult and reproach ; and he would give way—for no apparent reason—to fits of ungovernable fury. Withal I observed, that as we approached our destination, he manifested extreme uneasiness, and that his irritability towards us increased.

Having overheard so much relating to his intentions, and all along entertained suspicions of his ulterior design, I was fully prepared, upon our arrival at Messina, for the announcement he then made of a change of purpose. He now said he should go to Athens; the luggage would be sent forward; he would go and judge for himself whether it were better to settle there or at Messina, and then decide; so we set off for Piræus.

Of course I was not Questel's dupe. I believe that he saw this, and that it enraged him he could not shake me off. It was clearly his object to disarm our suspicions by affecting indecision respecting his plans of settlement, meanwhile drawing us nearer and nearer to Constantinople. I took care to put Ayesha upon her guard, who declared no power on earth should compel her to go thither, and that she would not leave me to proceed further alone with him.

We arrived at Piræus in the height of the sea-son, and put up at a small hotel near the sea-side. The little watering-place was overflowing with visitors from Athens and its vicinity, and we soon found ourselves surrounded by faces more or less familiar.

We had not been more than a couple of days here before my son-in-law boldly avowed his purpose of going to Constantinople and taking us with him. I told him very resolutely, but quietly, that neither I nor my daughter intended to journey any further in that direction, and that he might rest assured our decision was final. Ayesha was less calm. To his assertion of marital authority she opposed an open defiance; to his threats that he would assert his right to compel her—as his wife—to accompany him, she retorted by declaring she would resist violence by violence. As might be expected, her resolute opposition excited him to the highest pitch of fury, and, day after day, the most terrible altercations took place. He swore the most horrible oaths, threatened us with his vengeance, and, in fact, demeaned himself more like a maniac than a man in full possession of his senses; but all to no purpose. The result was the same. we were neither to be moved nor terrorized. Knowing, indeed, what we did, it was not likely we should yield to his wishes and fling ourselves headlong into the lion's mouth. On the other hand, he, with his mind fixed upon the prize promised for the betrayal of his wife into her father's hands — a prize now almost within his grasp — was equally unlikely to relinquish the pursuit of his object, so long as any means of accomplishing it remained untried. But the most extraordinary fact was, that, after his open avowal of his intention, he could delude himself with the idea of our trusting ourselves in his hands. I could account for such simplicity on his part only by the supposition that he hoped to rid himself somehow of my presence, then to inveigle Ayesha to Constantinople.

During ten days the scenes referred to continued. Our position became almost unendurable. My own was aggravated by the knowedge that my daughter was subjected to personal ill-treatment. I had, besides, to suffer the consequences of M. Questel's miserly arrangements at the hotel, and of his own selfishness. Only the remains of the meals served up for him came to my share, and I was otherwise accommodated in a manner which offered the very minimum of comfort or convenience. This treatment I knew to be premeditated, therefore I endured it, awaiting the end, and feeling that no remonstrance either on my part or Ayesha's would alter matters for the better.

All this time M. Questel was paying daily visits to Athens, going thither in the forenoon and returning in the evening. At length we learnt from himself the object of these mysterious journeys. He informed us, one morning, that he had been conferring about us and our affairs with the Turkish Ambassador and the French Consul, and that the former had assured him we should come to no harm if we went to Constantinople. He did not impart to us, what we afterwards learnt, that the latter had told him he would not be justified in attempting to convey his wife thither by force, for that no law gave him the right of compulsion over her. Finding we still declined to be charmed away by the smooth assurances of the Turkish Ambassador, especially coming second-hand through him, he surprised us with the intelligence that all the baggage had been sent forward direct to Constantinople from France, and as we could not go to that city, he intended proceeding thither himself.

I was not so greatly startled by this revelation, as I had, all along, been anticipating some such act of treachery. He gave us to understand, however, that he should not remain long absent. He would stay only a sufficient time to put matters in train for asserting our rights, upon the strength of the procuration he held, and return to report progress to us. As this arrangement suited us very well, it was agreed he should procure us a new abode, which having done, he handed me the key, gave his wife fifty francs, promising to send more, and without further leave-taking set out on his traitor's journey.

At that moment I knew he had at least twenty-five thousand francs about him, for before we left Paris, I had sewn the notes up in the lining of his coat. This amount was the balance remaining to him from the sale of his property in Brittany, after discharge of his debts.

We had not had the opportunity of inspecting the apartments he had retained for us. They were in a one-story house, situated in a remote suburb. The landlady, her husband, with two male and two female pledges of their affections, more than filled the upper floor. A room on the ground floor was occupied by a Greek and his partner: a veritable Xantippe, as we soon discovered. The remainder of the premises on the same level—two rooms and a kitchen—fell to our share.

If Monsieur Questel had purposely sought for us an abode where the extremes of penury and wretchedness were to be brought home to our apprehension in their most repulsive form, he could not have made a better selection. The house itself lay open to the thirty-two winds of heaven; neither doors nor windows closed, and the rain trickled down upon us on every side from the eaves. A cane-bottomed square couch and a straw palliasse did duty for one bed—my own—Ayesha being somewhat better accommodated. The scanty furniture was in the last stage of decrepitude and rickets, and as for the crockery, scarcely a piece was whole, and each owned a different origin.

I have referred to the tenants. Sincerely do I wish there had been no others than those I have mentioned; or, that the particular ones I do not care to name, and which so villanously tormented us, had been of a kind to be got rid of by a summary writ of ejectment. Flies of the most voracious nature and mosquitoes of the most bloodthirsty propensities, feasted upon our poor bodies at all hours; and what they left was gratefully accepted and duly appreciated by resident tribes of other flesh-puncturing insects whose legions successfully held their own, notwithstanding the exterminatory warfare we incessantly waged against them. As I had the strongest reasons for not making Ayesha acquainted with the exact condition of my purse, I determined—though I could have changed our abode—to remain in the lodgings the munificence of her husband had provided for us; at least until we heard from him.

We had been nearly a whole month in this horrible den before a letter came from Questel, whose advance had then long been exhausted. He sent a remittance of a hundred francs, and informed us he had seen Ayesha's father and her husband, Shevket. He said both were kindly disposed towards her, and would receive her kindly if she would go back, but that Kibrizli's animosity against me knew no bounds. He concluded by requesting us not to lay out any money upon furniture, and to expect him shortly to fetch us away.

Ayesha's eyes, were now, however, thoroughly opened to her husband's perfidy. I ought, perhaps, rather to say she had made up her mind to resent it. I had no need to prompt her to this decision, but I did my utmost in the way of exposition, to demonstrate the consistency of his course, from the first, with his ultimate object of inveigling us into the power of those we must unhappily regard as our worst enemies, notwithstanding they stood towards us in the relation of natural protectors.

To remain in our present dwelling was out of the question. We, therefore, changed lodgings and wrote to Questel, informing him of our removal, complaining of the insufficiency of his remittance, and urging pressing necessities as a plea for requesting an immediate and a more liberal supply of money. Three weeks elapsed before any reply came to this communication. It was to say he did not intend to remain in Constantinople, as he saw we were quite determined not to return to that city. He purposed now to settle at Kutaya, some three or four days' journey from Scutari. He would not send us any money then as he was about returning to Piræus, and would bring what was necessary, as also some handsome presents.

It occurred forcibly to me, upon receipt of this letter, that the moment had arrived for us to take a decisive step. Kutaya was too dangerously near to Scutari and Constantinople to render it an eligible abode for us, and Questel was manifestly seeking, in selecting it, to lure us within the grasp of the Turkish authorities. Perhaps he calculated that by keeping us pinched for means of living, sheer want would drive us to fall in with his plans;

or, perhaps, **he** still hoped to succeed in bamboozling **us, and that,** taken off our guard, we should fall into the trap he had so craftily set. He was doomed to be undeceived.

We answered Monsieur **Questel's** communication much as follows:

"MONSIEUR JEAN-MARIE QUESTEL,

"We do not want your handsome presents, **nor** money when you may choose to bring it We **are** in want of money now, at once. We wish **you** to understand we do not intend to go to Kutaya, nor to Constantinople. We are going back to Paris. You have played **the rogue** with us. You have left **us** without money; **you** have left us to **sleep** upon **straw**; you have not cared whether we starved. We have not the smallest confidence in you. All we ask you to do is to send us sufficient to pay **what** we owe here, and to defray our expenses to Paris. If you choose to rejoin us **there, you** will hear **of us** at the address of M. l'Abbé Boré. We shall expect an immediate reply to this letter."

This, however, was not precisely the fact. We **merely fancied** he might send us an answer, and we remained at Piræus long enough to test his intentions. But he never wrote, that we knew of, nor have we since seen or heard anything more of Jean-Marie Questel.

CHAPTER XVIII.

Changed demeanour of the Greeks towards us—Deceitful conduct of the French Vice-Consul—Attempt to inveigle us on board a Turkish war steamer—We are in danger from foot-pads—We receive an offer of a tour into the interior—Facts and inferences—We leave for Corfu.

OUR stay at Piræus after sending this message to Monsieur Questel, extended over about eight to ten days. Four would have amply sufficed to bring us an answer, in the ordinary course. I had decided to leave without unnecessary delay, for numerous incidents occurred, of minor importance in themselves, but which, taken together, satisfied me we were still objects of special attention to our friends at Constantinople.

I have stated, in an earlier chapter, that when offers of assistance were made to me by the Greek officials, on the occasion of my former visit, I declined to take advantage of them, because I knew they originated in a desire to annoy the authorities at Constantinople, and felt satisfied that when the war terminated, to the advantage of the Turks—as was certain—obsequiousness to the powers there would take the place of opposition. I was, therefore, not surprised to find we were now avoided rather than courted by our former friendly acquaintances. We were not positively tabooed, only perceptibly slighted. I might have failed to precise a circumstance to justify my challenging an explanation, but I could speak positively as to the change. Remembering the calumnies against us set afloat in Paris, by agents, official and others, acting under instructions from my husband and his *entourage,* I concluded that similar influences were active in creating a prejudice against us in the social circles in which we were now moving. We were constantly dogged by low Turks, who would mutter curses at us as they passed, calling us Giaours and other infamous names. These incidents alarmed me, for I knew that Turks were capable of carrying their vindictiveness to any extreme against their co-religionists guilty of infidelity to Mahomet, and for this offence Ayesha was marked, and I likewise, being regarded as the cause of her apostacy.

I also noticed a great intimacy between the Turkish Ambassador and the French Vice-Consul, who arrived at Piræus from Athens shortly after the departure of M. Questel for Constantinople. They came to pass a time at the sea-side. The Vice-Consul was quite new in the service and ambitious of acquiring influence. This he could do only by currying favour with the Turkish Ambassador. Now, our history was well known, and he could not but be aware of the desire of the Ottoman officials at the seat of Government to get us back, and of the policy of their representatives abroad, to promote that object. I therefore, and naturally enough, regarded with a degree of suspicion, the constant interchange of visits and presents between the Vice-Consul and the Ambassador; and my mistrust of the former became decided when I heard that he had received the Cross of the Order of the Medjidi, although he had not rendered any service whatever to the Porte, that I could discover. Nevertheless, I strove to believe I deceived myself, for he paid us two or three visits, and seemed to sympathize with us in our unfortunate position.

The time came when his sincerity was to be put to the test. The regular Corfu steamer was to sail within a few days, and I had decided to go by it, my intention being to proceed to Trieste, and thence to Vienna, where I hoped to prevail upon the Ambassador, an old acquaintance of mine, to support a petition in our favour to the Grand Vizier, Ali Pasha. I was short of funds for the journey, and for the discharge of our small liabilities, but did not like to apply to the Turkish Ambassador, a Greco-Turk, lest he should refuse help on the plea that I had only to return to Constantinople to be placed beyond want. Presuming, therefore, upon the Vice-Consul's professions of interest, I waited upon him and submitted my case. Nothing could be more polite than his reception, only, he said he could not give me any money until next morning, if I would do him the favour of calling. Quite satisfied now that I had misjudged him, I withdrew, thanking him most sincerely. Next day I waited upon him, according to appointment, and was informed he had left, unexpectedly, an hour or two before, and had gone a journey into the interior.

This was certainly a startling and an unpleasant piece of intelligence, not calculated to allay my suspicions, which returned with tenfold force. Why this deliberate deception? I could not comprehend it, and turned from his threshhold, indignant and disgusted.

Another singular incident occurred that same evening.

A war steamer, bearing the Ottoman flag, lay in

the port. She was intended to convey the Turkish Ambassador to Corfu to attend the ceremonial of the baptism of the Prince Royal of Greece. Her captain and her officers were Turks of the fanatical school, imbued with the hereditary traditions of their race against the Giaour and all apostates from the faith of the Prophet. They were frequenters of the public promenade, and generally kept pretty closely behind us. We could hear their remarks upon us, which were not complimentary. They could not reconcile themselves to seeing Ayesha—a girl of high birth, a descendant of the Prophet, the daughter of a great minister—appear openly amongst the Giaours, with her face unveiled. It was a scandal upon the religion they professed; an unpardonable iniquity. The proper place for the daughter of Kibrizli Mehemet Pasha was Constantinople, with her relatives, not with the Giaours. Of all this, as it came from time to time, not a word was lost upon me. My astonishment may be conceived, when, on the evening referred to, the Captain suddenly, and for the first time, addressed me on the promenade, and after a few preliminary, unmeaning, complimentary phrases, offered me and my daughter a free passage on board his vessel to Corfu. As I had spoken only to the French Consul of my intention to go to that city, there could be no doubt of the source whence the Captain had derived his information. This fact at once placed me upon my guard; and Ayesha let me perceive that she also regarded the proposition with disfavour. I remembered, also, that the secretary to the Turkish Ambassador, whom we met frequently upon the promenade, and with whom we were on very good how-do-you-do terms, had more than once hinted—of course under instructions—that as we would not go to Constantinople, we ought to go to London: and, also, that the same suggestion had been made by the French Consul. Coupling these facts together, and the Captain's unexpected offer, I came to the conclusion that if I accepted it, the probabilities were, I should never see either London or Corfu. I therefore declined it, and believe that in doing so I avoided a snare. This, too, was the first time Ayesha appeared to have had an instinctive perception of danger. Nor were our apprehensions ill-founded.

Our residence was situated in one of the suburbs. One evening, some three or four days after the departure of the French Consul, we had remained unusually late on the public promenade. It was a lovely moonlight night, and Ayesha had entreated me to delay our return home, so we outstaid all the promenaders. The way to our house, which stood in a retired spot, lay through a small alley of trees; and as we approached it, I suddenly perceived the dark figures of two men gliding behind the trees bordering the path. They saw us, and stopped when we did. It was not absolutely necessary, except to make a short cut, for us to go through the alley, and, having calmed Ayesha, I proposed to skirt it until we reached the more open road, near by which stood the residence of the French Consul. As we moved, the men moved, still endeavouring to hide themselves. I now felt convinced we were the objects of their sinister intentions. I began to be seriously alarmed; for there appeared to me to be equal danger whether we proceeded or turned back. Happily, our anxiety was removed by the appearance of two police agents, coming from the city, under whose protection we placed ourselves. One of them conducted us home; the other succeeded in preventing the escape of the men until his comrade rejoined him, when they were both captured. Next morning they were brought to us. They could not render a satisfactory account of themselves, nor of their object in prowling about at that spot at so late an hour; and as they were recognized as belonging to the very worst of the low classes which infest the environs of Athens, they were imprisoned as vagabonds.

These rascals may have been mere vulgar footpads, bent upon robbery only; but I had the strongest suspicions that a more sinister purpose actuated them, for the accomplishment of which the locality and the late hour afforded them every facility. Assassination was by no means rare, and when political considerations were in question, the police authorities became, under the inspiration of the government officials, unusually obtuse, even to the most obvious facts.

It was an odd circumstance, too, that on this same evening, upon meeting on the promenade the secretary of the Turkish Ambassador, he again advised me to go to London without delay, adding that if I would call next morning, he had something more to say. Of course, I complied with his request. He then placed in my hands a hundred and fifty francs, saying they were from the Ambassador, towards my expenses to London. The donation was as welcome as the hint to go to England was unpleasant. I accepted the one with thanks, but held my peace upon the subject of the destination I might select. The suggestion, coming from such a quarter, was of itself sufficient to cause me to receive it with suspicion.

The steamer for Corfu was to leave the next day, early in the forenoon, and I at once took places in it. I disposed of my very small remnant of valuables, and of sundry articles of wearing apparel—in our position luxurious—and with the proceeds discharged our liabilities; but I did not intimate to anyone that I intended to leave. My reasons for silence must be obvious.

In the evening, I and my daughter were taking refreshments at one of the open-air *cafés* on the promenade, when two gentlemen came up; one, an acquaintance and a friend of the Turkish Ambassador's Secretary, the other an individual we had frequently seen in the company of the French Vice-Consul and of the French Admiral on the station, who, I may add, we heard had accompanied his political colleague on his little journey into the interior. He turned out to be the Admiral's Secretary, and was presented by our other friend as extremely desirous of making our acquaintance.

The usual unmeaning conversational aperients having been exhausted, Mr. Secretary brought round the conversation to the subject of our de-

s

parture, and considerably astonished me by expressing his regret that we had not accepted the offer of the Captain of the war steamer to convey us to Corfu. I did not perceive how my refusal could possibly concern Mr. Secretary, nor what interest he could take in our movements; but I presently found he had sought us out to submit a proposal on his own account. It was to take myself and Ayesha a tour of some eight or ten days in the environs of Athens. He would show us everything worth seeing, and defray all expenses. We should benefit by the change of scene; the journey would be a succession of delightful surprises; would, in fact, enchant us; and he declared he would not take a denial.

Of course, I could make but one reply to this unexpected and singularly ill-timed proposition. I declined it, without giving any reason. But Mr. Secretary was so persistent, I found I could not easily shake him off. The advanced state of our preparations for leaving, urged as one reason for refusing his offer, would, he said, facilitate our going with him all the sooner. Had we already taken out our tickets for Corfu? They could be cancelled, and he would renew them, or make an arrangement for the extension of the date. In a word, his **importunity** left me without argument or excuse; **for I had** the **best reasons for** keeping my intended departure secret, or I might have urged the fact as a decisive objection. I satisfied **him** at last by making an appointment to see him **next day** at two o'clock, **to receive my final answer.** As he did not know **I already had our passage-tickets in my pocket, and the rendezvous was for an hour** considerably **later** than **that** at which the steamer **started, he** probably left under the impression that **my** reply would be affirmative. I should not, under any circumstances, have entertained such a proposition, notwithstanding that Ayesha, intent upon change **and pleasure, did not** see any impropriety in accepting it, nor suspect the risks we might incur **in surrendering** our movements **to the** control of a **stranger, whom we knew to be** intimately associated with **our enemies and** their allies. The recompense of eight thousand pounds to whomsoever should restore Ayesha **into** the hands of **her** father, **was** sufficiently large to induce unscrupulous **persons to attempt her** abduction **by force** or by **fraud, to which I was the only** obstacle. To wit: the Captain **of the Turkish war steamer** might easily have whisked **us** off to Constantinople, had we trusted ourselves on board his vessel, and advancement as well as money would probably have rewarded so bold a stroke. Again, if the author of the last proposition contemplated treachery, nothing was easier than to arrange an attack upon us in the wild districts around Athens, leaving me to be ransomed, or to my fate, whilst Ayesha was being conveyed away. Real occurrences of this kind were far from uncommon: and a sham capture of us by sham Greek brigands, for a sufficient bribe, presented no difficulty.

My suspicions may have been ill-founded, and I am conscious that many persons may regard me as influenced by a morbid tendency to ascribe evil intentions where none of the kind exist. On the other hand, I may urge my experience of treachery, when I had not suspected any, as a complete answer to such a theory, and as a full justification of myself, even if I have taken alarm at only imaginary dangers, and exaggerated simple circumstances into undue importance. In recording actual facts, I must leave the reader to determine how far they harmonize with ascribed motives.

I cannot, for instance, affirm that the Captain of the Turkish war-steamer, who might have taken us to Constantinople instead of Corfu; that the French Admiral's secretary, who might have effected, in the manner suggested, my detention and Ayesha's abduction; that the two footpads, who could not have any but a sinister object in view in waylaying us and might easily have disposed of me and borne off my daughter, were acting under common instructions. Nor could I say that the course of the French Consul was in pursuance of some ulterior design of his own. Nevertheless, the facts were these: we were waylaid by footpads, and were in absolute peril from them; the French Consul had an interest in cultivating the favour of the Turkish officials; he broke a special appointment of his own making with me, and set out, unexpectedly to everybody, on a journey into the interior of a country notoriously unsafe; the French Admiral accompanied him, leaving his secretary free; almost simultaneously with their departure, the Secretary proposed to take us a tour into the very region to which his superior and the Consul were reported to be gone; the Consul and the Turkish Ambassador were in constant and close communication; a large reward awaited him who should take my daughter back to Constantinople, with me or without me; further, the fact of the offer of this reward was notorious in the circles in which we moved. In presence of these facts, the inference seems conclusive that plans for our abduction, by some means, were in contemplation, and that several parties were interested in carrying them out.

Early next morning we went on board the steamer; and if the Admiral's Secretary kept the appointment I made with him, he probably soon arrived at the conclusion that we were, at that hour, well on our way to Corfu.

CHAPTER XIX.

From Corfu to Trieste—Haida Effendi's strange request—He is baffled—We reach Trieste—Visits to Haida Effendi—His proposals—How we got to Paris.

We hired a furnished apartment at Corfu in a house situated near the sea. Shortly after our arrival, the infant Prince Royal of Greece was christened in the cathedral church of Saint Spiridion. We received through an anonymous source, tickets to witness the ceremonial, which was grand and imposing, and attracted a numerous and distinguished company, amongst which we recognized many familiar faces.

We were not interfered with in any way during our stay at Corfu, which lasted about four weeks, whence I concluded that the proofs we had recently given of vigilance over ourselves, had induced those who so pertinaciously pursued us to change their tactics, and leave us quiet for a time. One circumstance, nevertheless, struck me as singular, and sufficiently significant.

The Turkish Consul—upon whom I called, and afterwards met several times—taking up the cue of his colleagues at Piræus—pressed me to go to London, saying that Musurus Bey had great power, and would certainly be able to obtain something for us. He even expressed surprise that we had come to Corfu, and added that he knew we had received money towards our expenses to England. On the last occasion I told him the lack of sufficient funds precluded us from travelling, save by stages, to any place whatever, whereupon he gave me a hundred francs to help us on to Trieste, still urging us, however, to proceed to London.

I had no desire to remain any time at Trieste, my object being to reach Vienna as soon as possible. The Turkish Consul—a Greek—met my application for means to go forward, by saying he must telegraph to Vienna for instructions. I had presented Ayesha to him in her true name—that is, as the daughter of Kibrizli-Mehemet Pasha—but represented myself as her companion. I requested him not to mention me in his telegram, for as I entertained the conviction that the separation of myself and daughter was contemplated—though of course I did not disclose my reason to him —I thought it would be more prudent, under actual circumstances, to keep myself in the background.

The reply came in due course. It was, to send Ayesha on, if alone, and in such case to advance just sufficient to defray her travelling expenses to Vienna. The Consul—a highly honourable, worthy man—expressed considerable astonishment at this answer, and commented warmly upon the indecorum of his superior's course; he himself being struck with the impropriety of Ayesha's travelling alone, and placing herself in the hands of the Ambassador. I had my own opinion of the matter, but kept it to myself.

In answer to my request for an advance upon the sum specified for my daughter's expenses, in order to enable me to accompany her, he said his general orders rendered his compliance with my request impossible, save at the risk of consequences for disobeying instructions. I suggested a compromise as a solution of the dilemma. He advanced me forty francs, and I placed in his hands a velvet paletot, as security, giving him an acknowledgment of the loan, he returning me a receipt for the article deposited. He then telegraphed that Ayesha would leave by a particular train, but of course omitted the fact of her travelling with a companion.

On our arrival at the station at Vienna, I observed the Ambassador's carriage in waiting, and a servant on the look-out for somebody. We passed on, and proceeded to the Hôtel du Lion d'Or. Next morning we made our call upon Haida Effendi, who received us with a profusion of compliments, and with every manifestation of pleasure. If he was astonished at seeing me, he did not betray himself; nor did I touch upon the subject I knew he must be desirous to avoid. It sufficed for me to know, that my presence was unwelcome, and had baffled his object in wishing Ayesha to come alone.

Haida Effendi was at this time about forty-five years of age. I had known him in the time of my prosperity, when he was quite a lad, and used to run of errands for me. His father, one of the old Jannissaries, was head tailor of the Sultan's harem; but his mother neglected him for a new-born child, and he was left to the tender mercies of the Providence which regulates the destinies of vagabonds. He was an ugly little elf, but sharp, talented, and of a kind disposition. He was also sufficiently philosophical to put up patiently with occasional rough usage, to wear coarse clothes, and in a word, to endure the thousand and one petty miseries of a dependent upon the stranger's bounty. By degrees he educated himself, and having been brought under the notice of Ali Pasha, the great minister encouraged him, and ultimately employed him in a subordinate capacity at the Ministère of Foreign Affairs. Having now more leisure and favourable opportunities, he soon acquired a mastery of the Persian, Arabic, French, and other languages, and was finally appointed to the higher offices of his department. His nomination to the post of full Ambassador to Vienna was only a suitable reward for so much perseverance, and for his devotion to the policy of Ali Pasha.

Haida Effendi invited us to stay and breakfast with him, and in the course of conversation adverted to our journey. I could see he seemed embarrassed to explain his strange request for Ayesha to be sent forward, if alone, and I felt that he could not let the incident pass unnoticed. He brought the explanation about presently, by expressing his regret at our having been missed, on our arrival, by his domestics. The fact was they were looking out for only one lady, which accounted for us two having passed unnoticed. He had instructed the Consul to send on Ayesha, if alone, because he was not certain her husband might not be with her, and he did not wish to see that personage.

Now, this was a very lame excuse, for my diplomatic friend must have known that Ayesha's husband was at Constantinople. I did not, however, permit him to perceive that I discredited his explanation, especially in the teeth of his reiterated assurances of the great pleasure it had afforded him to see me arrive with my daughter. I none the less clung to the conviction that some secret reason had prompted his request to the Consul. Nor was I mistaken.

Our position and the condition of our affairs at Constantinople, naturally occupied the attention of our friend, whose influence with his patron, Ali Pasha, we were most anxious to secure, and hoped he would not refuse to exercise in our favour. He promised, unhesitatingly, to do this, but suggested that it depended solely upon ourselves not to require any appeal to Ali Pasha, nor to anyone else. If we pleased, a position of independence might be secured for us in Europe; yes, even in Vienna. In fact—not to prolong this recital by unnecessary details—he ended by proposing to marry Ayesha, whose independence he would secure by a handsome settlement. He left the table to fetch a quantity of diamonds which he set before her, saying he would ive her these and many more, if she would consent to his proposition. He would devote himself to secure her happiness; would take her to Constantinople, and her father, seeing her re-married to one of her own race and religion, would be pacified, and not interfere with her any more. As for me, if I too would go back, I should be greatly benefited; if not, he would not trouble himself about what might happen to me.

In making this proposition, Haida Effendi—who had a wife at Constantinople whom I knew—had not the remotest idea he was outraging us. He treated us in Vienna as he would have treated us in Constantinople. His notions of the social relations between the sexes were strictly Oriental, and as in our country such an offer could be made and accepted without impropriety. I must candidly confess our sense of delicacy was not so much shocked by it as it ought to have been, and as it no doubt would have been, but for our Eastern education and habits: a striking illustration of the demoralizing tendency of Turkish institutions. In Turkey, indeed, marriage and divorce are reduced absolutely to their simplest forms. With regard to the latter, both parties enjoy equal privileges, the penalty on the one side being the obligation to provide for the partner the husband has repudiated, and on the other, the forfeiture by the wife seeking a separation, of her right to any provision for her future maintenance.

Ayesha regarded his **Excellency's** proposal in the light of a device, a trick, and said so bluntly, adding that she could place no kind of confidence in any one who talked to her of going back to Constantinople. All she wanted was her liberty, and an allowance from her father, sufficient to enable her to live comfortably. If his Excellency would intercede to obtain it for her, he would earn her gratitude for life.

My old friend reiterated his promise to communicate with Ali Pasha, and when we took leave, gave me five hundred francs to meet our present requirements, and invited us to dine with him next day. He entertained us in magnificent Oriental style, but renewed his overtures of the previous day with a like result; only, that this time I gave him to understand he must not again subject us to the same importunities.

During the remainder of our stay, which lasted about a week, we visited Haida Effendi several times. On the last occasion he urged me to adopt a suggestion he had more than once made, that we should establish ourselves in a shop, to be stocked with Turkish perfumes and fancy articles of Oriental origin, his opinion being that the novelty of the enterprise and the beauty of the younger vendor, would attract a large amount of custom. I dare say he was right. No doubt the speculation would have succeeded, but I had no fancy for trading upon my daughter's attractions. I told my friend I should prefer hiring a house, but he raised so many objections to this course that I gave in. The only question was one of money. He settled it at once by placing in my hands five hundred florins in notes, towards the expenses of the projected establishment, expressing his regret that, owing to the influence of my husband, he durst not assist me materially by making me a permanent allowance. This I understood, but although I accepted his gift, I could not make up my mind to carry out the project he had suggested, notwithstanding that upon quitting him, he fully believed my intention was to do so.

I may confess I entertained serious apprehensions of protracting our stay in Vienna, and as the means of quitting it without delay seemed to have fallen into my hands as if from some providential source, I turned the whole matter over in my mind that same night, and decided to start for Paris by the earliest train. Sharp practice, some will say, but in my case the most prudent course.

Upon our arrival in Paris, I wrote to him, explaining matters, adding expressions of regret that the very peculiar circumstances in which we were placed, rendered it impossible for us to carry out his suggestion; but as his desire was to serve us, we thought he would approve of our decision to turn his gift to account in Paris, where we felt ourselves in greater surety than in Vienna. In due course we received a reply, thanking us for our excellent wishes for his prosperity, and calling our attention to an enclosure from Ali Pasha. This letter, couched in the most amicable terms, intimated that he could not interfere between us and the person respecting whom we had written, so long as we remained absent from Constantinople, for the latter was simply mad upon the subject; but if we would return, he, on his side, promised to assist us to the utmost extent of his power. As, however, we had decided not to go back to the Turkish capital, Ali Pasha's good offices were never called into requisition. To conclude the episode of this my last visit to Vienna, I may add that upon the death of Ali Pasha, his *protégé* Haida Effendi was disgraced and exiled to Mitylene, where, by the strangest of chances, he occupied the very house in which I and my daughter had resided during my own banishment. Whatever the ostensible reason given for his exile, the real cause was his marriage with a German lady—a governess—in Vienna, whose European manners, especially her custom of going out unveiled, scandalized Turkish society far more than his repudiation of his first wife, after a married life of over twenty years.

Before we left Vienna, the paletot I had left in the hands of the Turkish Consul at Trieste, was returned to me. Whether his superior reimbursed him the advance of forty francs made to me upon it, as security, I know not. I do know that Haida Effendi wrote him a very sharp letter for not giving me the money, and for taking the garment in pledge; but I am quite sure it would have been a much sharper one had the good-hearted, perhaps, over-timid Consul followed his own inclination, and paid my expenses to Vienna, as well as my daughter's.

CHAPTER XX.

Conversations with Haida Effendi upon matters personal to myself.

BEFORE I take final leave in these pages of my friend Haida Effendi, it behoves me to record, in a summarized form, sundry conversations I had with him on the subject of those events—only slightly referred to in my former volume—which, on account of their fatal influence over my fortunes, merit serious notice, and also because they have been purposely misrepresented to my detriment. I need scarcely say that they relate to the causes of my separation from the Pasha, my husband. Apart from their immediate bearing upon this narrative, they will forcibly illustrate the peculiar character of Turkish society.

Haida Effendi—like the majority of his official colleagues—had the slenderest knowledge of the occurrences which led to my disgrace and exile; and although, as he assured me, knowing me so intimately, he gave no ear to the disparaging statements industriously circulated against me, he felt anxious, nevertheless, to be made acquainted with the facts from an authoritative source.

The charge of encompassing a cold-blooded murder is a heavy one to lie under. Where mystery accompanies the crime, and the scene of it is in a distant land, it is difficult for the party incriminated to vindicate himself, though wholly innocent, especially where special pains are taken to fix it upon him, by concealing the circumstances which establish the improbability of his guilt. This has been my case; wherefore I may claim to plead my own cause without seeking an excuse at the hands of the reader.

Bessir, the Nubian eunuch, who was murdered by Fatmah and her paramour Omer, was a lad of about thirteen, and a great favourite with me, because attached to my personal service, which afforded me the opportunity of appreciating his fidelity and his many other qualities. He was unpopular with all his fellow domestics and slaves, for the one reason that he resented their calling me Giaour, and rebuked them for speaking otherwise disrespectfully of me. Fatmah was jealous of him, and hated him because he noted and reported her thefts and other misdoings, and because he knew of her shameless profligacy, not only with Omer the Turk, but with other servants of the household. She, too, was disliked by her colleagues; and they—with a view to get rid of her—encouraged Bessir to watch and report her movements to me, believing that I should discharge her. The other two eunuchs, Bessir's elders, were also jealous of him, because he enjoyed my confidence, and was continually receiving marks of my favour. These rival and stormy elements in a household such as ours, could not fail some day to come into open collision, even had they been left undisturbed; but they were constantly wrought upon by an outward influence not yet mentioned.

My husband had many near male relatives in Constantinople and in Cyprus—of which island it may be remembered he was a native—who were looking forward to inherit his wealth, and were therefore enraged when they learnt that a son had been born to him at Belgrade. Whether they—for some half-dozen were in the Pasha's suite—actually bribed Fatmah to act as she did, or held out promises of a considerable share of the inheritance, if it should come to them in consequence of the death of this child, or of any doubt being thrown upon his legitimacy, certain it is, she originated rumours of this kind, which, however, deceived no one, and acquired consistency only after the event occurred I am about more particularly to refer to. They had also gained over the intendant of my household—a Turk—by promises of a high post; for men in subordinate, even menial positions, not unfrequently rise to be ministers through some intrigue of this sort, and as he was very ambitious, corruption did its work with him, and he became the leader of the hostile band in my own house.

It may appear puerile to enter into the minute details of the strictly domestic circle, but the reader is requested to bear in mind that a great abyss separates an Eastern from a Western household; and that, more frequently than is suspected, changes and revolutions which overturn dynasties in the East, as also tragedies of the most appalling character, involving whole families in life-long misery, may be traced to some wretched intrigue in that nest of iniquity and demoralization, the harem.

Another element in this unfortunate affair was the political one. Kibrizli had become a power in the country. Reschid-Pasha, Grand Vizier, and Fétih-Pasha his friend, private secretary to the Sultan, and also brother-in-law to him, were my particular friends, and for this reason alone became my husband's patrons. My friendship with them had commenced long antecedent to their attainment of ministerial authority. On the same side were Ali Pasha, Minister of Foreign Affairs, and Rusti-Mehemet-Pasha, Minister of War. Opposed to these were Mehemet Ali-Pasha, Minister of Marine, and another brother-in-law of the Sultan's; Riza-Pasha, an ex-minister of Abdul Mejid's, and the reputed intimate friend of the Valideh-Sultan; Rifed-Pasha, President of the Council; the Valideh-Sultan herself; Mehemet-Pasha, Minister of Justice, and Basha, the chief eunuch of the Sultan. The one object this tribe of opponents had in view, and for which they steadily intrigued, was to destroy the influence of my husband and of his patrons, and as it was notorious that he owed his position to my old intimacy with Reschid and Fétih Pasha, their special immediate aim, during his absence on his embassy in London, was to depreciate me by whatever means. The reports set afloat by Fatmah were, of course, known to them, through the domestics of their own households, but up to the time mentioned, no opportunity had presented itself to turn these rumours to account against me.

I have already stated, and I again affirm the fact, that it was with my husband's full knowledge and consent, the substitution of another child for Mustapha-Djehad, in the event of the decease of the latter—imminent at any moment—was to be made, the object being to secure to me, Ayesha and the lad, the wealth which, in default of direct male issue to the Pasha, would be divided amongst a horde of rapacious male relatives of his, who did not care for him, and who would not have given him a crown piece to save him from starvation.

We had agreed upon our course before the Pasha left for London; whilst there he received frequent intelligence of the child's critical condition, and when, upon the physician's report, he was informed that no hope of the boy's recovery remained, his reply was quite decisive, and left me no alternative but to carry out his last instructions. His wish was my law. If Mustapha-Djehad died, then another son was to be born to the Pasha; that was all.

But Djehad did not die, and the infant who would —in the contrary case—have taken his place, remained with his nurse, shut up in Fatmah's apartments.

The Pasha had been away about eight months when Djehad's intended successor appeared upon the scene. Any gossip relating to the affair was confined to the slaves, from whom concealment was impossible, but whose testimony was worth nothing. I awaited the issue without the smallest anxiety, for I knew that the Pasha would, in due time, determine whether the infant introduced by Fatmah should be retained and taken care of, or be restored to its own parents. Strange to say, a political incident in which I was not the least concerned, brought about the catastrophe.

Reschid Pasha, anxious to consolidate his power, cherished the design of marrying his favourite son, Ali Galup Pasha, to Fatmah-Sultan, the eldest daughter of the Sultan Abdul-Mejid; in accomplishing which object he ultimately succeeded. The other ministers, however, opposed this design, and Reschid, with a view to strengthen himself with a new ally, determined to recall my husband from London, and give him the portfolio of Foreign Affairs. The fact soon became known, and immediately all our enemies were on the alert.

The ground had—as it unfortunately happened—been only too well prepared for their operations, and circumstances favoured their designs. The old outstanding feud between Fatmah and Bessir had augmented in intensity to such a degree, that one day they came to a hand-to-hand conflict, which, had the combatants not been separated, would certainly have resulted in a murder. Their quarrels became so frequent and terrible, and their threats of inflicting personal violence on each other assumed so practical and desperate a form, that I found it absolutely indispensable to send Fatmah away. I made her a present of a sum equivalent to forty pounds sterling, and bade her return when the Pasha came back, who would determine the question of restoring her to her place in the household, or of making a suitable provision for her. After a protracted discussion she agreed to adopt my suggestion, and went to Pera, where she took up her abode in the family of a major in the Turkish army. When, however, the news of my husband's promotion to his new ministerial office was conveyed to her, her cupidity was excited by the prospect of being reinstated in her former position, in a grander household, and with enlarged opportunities of peculation.

For my own part, I had no intention of again receiving this astute, wicked woman into my house. I had even conferred with my intendant concerning the best mode of satisfying her, and of inducing her to go back into her own country. I did not then know he was in close league with our secret foes, the relatives of Kibrizli, and was at that very moment in constant communication with Fatmah, urging her to return to the house, and risk my displeasure; his object being to bring her and Bessir once more into collision.

She made her re-appearance in it on the occasion of the feast given in honour of Ayesha's first reading of the Koran in public—as stated in my former volume—and resolutely refused to leave it again. I communicated my fears of a renewal of the quarrels between the two rivals and enemies, but my intendant laughed at me, and endeavoured to satisfy me that their mutual threats of murder were only empty words. They quarrelled and made it up constantly: nothing came of it. Yet at this time he was inciting Bessir against Fatmah, and Fatmah against Bessir, and urging their fellow-servants to do the same.

This fact—with many others—did not come to light immediately, but in the course of the judicial inquiry which followed the event now to be spoken of.

It was important to those I must call the conspirators, to provoke a public scandal before my husband's return. They knew him too well to be under any kind of delusion as to what his course would be towards the detractors of his wife and his own self. Any attempt on their part to procure an investigation into the truth of the report in circulation concerning the legitimacy of Mustapha-Djehad would be at once crushed, and the parties summarily punished, perhaps disposed of. If, however, by any means, fair or foul, the interference of the police authorities could be secured, their immediate object would be gained. The deadly feud between Fatmah and Bessir suggested a diabolical means of achieving it, and these two became unconscious instruments in the hands of the conspirators. Whether Fatmah killed Bessir, or Bessir killed Fatmah, the origin of the deed was to be attributed to me, the ostensible reason for the crime being the silencing of an inconvenient witness to the alleged illegitimacy of Mustapha-Djehad. Under such circumstances, the judicial authorities must investigate the crime, and the motives for it, and in all probability would examine the question of legitimacy. This was what the conspirators desired. The reported recall of my husband by Reschid Pasha, in furtherance—as I have already stated—of his ambitious views for his favourite son, stimulated the parties into activity, and quickened their perceptions for opportunities of accomplishing that sinister design.

When Fatmah returned to the house she had been one month absent, and five had elapsed since the introduction of the infant of which I was to have assumed the maternity. Misled by my intendant's assurances of the harmlessness of the feud between this woman and Bessir, and disinclined to interfere again—in the anticipation of my husband's return—I took no steps, as I might have done, to remove Fatmah by force, or to place the matter in the hands of the police authorities. I contented myself with laying strict injunctions upon both parties to confine themselves to their own quarters, and for a few days the peace of the household was not disturbed. It proved to be the calm before the tempest.

It was the period of the festival of the Ramazan, when it is customary to keep open house, and mutual invitations to eat, drink, and be merry, are the order of the day. On these occasions the suites of the great folks interchange similar courtesies, and an invitation to the slaves of one household to attend a feast at another, is considered as an act of special politeness to the owner of those slaves, because, though these alone benefit by it, the civility is intended for the master, and is so acknowledged. My intendant, taking advantage of this custom, solicited my permission to invite my slaves to a feast at his house, to meet the slaves of some other households. This was within a week after Fatmah's return. Nothing suspecting, I consented, though I should be inconvenienced by their absence, as I myself entertained that same day a considerable company. Instead, however, of conducting them to his house, he concealed them in a large stable on our premises contiguous to the bath-room, where they found the domestics of the house, and the Cyprus men of the Pasha's suite, his relatives, already hidden: in all, fourteen of them. This was at about five in the afternoon.

Why, all this mystery? Why this gathering?

Early that morning, one of the male domestics made a singular revelation to his comrades. Passing along the dark corridor leading to the men's quarters, he saw Fatmah at the door giving access to them. She was whispering loudly to some one on the other side, who turned out to be her paramour Omer. The words she uttered were:

"Send him to me, to the bath-room, and we will settle him. Mind, you are to help me."

It was an easy matter to decoy Bessir to the bath-room, where his services were constantly in requisition. At the appointed hour—just about sun-down—and at a preconcerted signal, Omer told the lad somebody wanted him there, and he proceeded at once on the errand. Scarcely had the door opened than he found himself a prisoner in the powerful grasp of Fatmah, a woman of immense strength, a match for any man, and in whose hands the poor eunuch, weak and sickly as are all of his caste, was as a hind in the claws of a tiger. He struggled, nevertheless, and turned to flee, when he was confronted by Omer. Throttled by Fatmah, dragged to the water-tap by Omer, and the water turned upon him, his poor life was soon extinguished. Omer returned to his quarters, and Fatmah, having locked the door of the bath-room, made her way back to the harem.

. I was in the midst of my friends, exerting myself to the utmost to entertain them, when the awful words: "Bessir is dead!" were uttered in a whisper in my ear. I looked round and beheld Fatmah!

"Bessir dead?" I shrieked. "Then you have murdered him!" I could say no more, for I lost consciousness.

The commotion amongst the guests was terrible, as soon as my words were circulated. Some surrounded me; some ran one way, others another. One of my slaves, who held the rank of Treasurer, sped to what was called the treasure-chamber, for a restorative, not observing she was closely followed by Fatmah, nor that Fatmah made good use of the opportunity to seize from an open casket a necklace of large pearls with a diamond clasp, worth some thousands of pounds, which she tucked under her arm and disappeared with, though only for the moment, as she was presently stopped by the slaves on her way out.

The commotion without equalled that within. Omer had been caught, and was being beaten in the court-yard by three negro slaves, armed with staves. The others, similarly provided, headed by my Intendant, and one Achmed-Effendi, a relative of my husband's, invaded the harem in a tumultuous body; an outrageous act, and an offence, the enormity of which is not to be appreciated by persons unfamiliar with Eastern customs. Fatmah, in the midst of them, was dragged and hustled, thrown to the ground and beaten, her assailants urging her, with loud shouts and menaces of death, to declare I had ordered her to commit the crime. At last—after receiving terrible punishment, and I believe to save herself from being beaten or trampled to death—she accused me.

I stood aghast, but said nothing. I could not understand what was passing before me. I saw that I stood in imminent peril, and that an imprudence in word or deed might cost me my life. I began to comprehend something, only when the wretches from Cyprus, my husband's own relatives, whose benefactress I was, surrounded me and exclaimed:

"Ah! you want to secure the Pasha's property. But the children are not yours. They are not the Pasha's children. Ah! you shall see whether we will let ourselves be cheated!"

It is needless, as I am merely reiterating the principal incidents of this crime, to relate in detail what followed: how a general rummage of my effects took place by this mob of ruffians, each taking what came nearest to his hand; how the women of the establishment also helped themselves, and how I came off with only a remnant of my jewels and other valuables. All these facts came out in the course of the inquiry that followed, but the issue of which, so far as concerned my acquittal of any participation in the murder of my unfortunate eunuch, I do not to this day know. I only know that Fatmah was banished to her own country, and that Omer was condemned to ten years' imprisonment.

I have no need to seek to exculpate myself from the accusation of having instigated this crime. I will merely say I had no interest so dreadful an act could promote, and had I contemplated its commission to serve any purpose whatsoever, I could have accomplished the removal of the poor lad, as indeed of any one of my own slaves, without awakening suspicion, and especially without creating a public scandal. The facts speak for themselves, and I leave my vindication to them.

My husband did not return to Constantinople until five months after this lugubrious event. I wished to see him, and he desired to see me, for his affection for me at that time was unaltered. But we were prevented from meeting, so that I never had the opportunity of an explanation with him, although I had the satisfaction of knowing he was satisfied of my innocence. Then, our relations, were changed. I was already his divorced wife.

It was represented to my husband whilst he was still in London, that this affair had created so great a scandal, not only in the country but abroad, on account of the implication in it of his wife, no alternative remained to him of maintaining his position, but to divorce me. To this suggestion he would not listen, until, after several communications, it was finally urged upon him that, unless he took this step, he would lose the support of Reschid Pasha and his party, and be relegated into obscurity. My husband, who had risen to eminence from the humblest position, no doubt shrank from the sacrifice his definite refusal to comply with this last intimation would entail, and yielded.

The political opposition to him may be briefly explained. As a man of influence, a minister, and one of the supporters of Reschid Pasha, to discredit him in public opinion was to bring into disrepute those with whom he was associated. Reschid—strong as he was—could not sustain a colleague, over whose wife hung the infamy of a great public scandal. By divorcing me, though against his inclination, he placed himself on the side of his enemies, clamouring for my disgrace, and deprived them of a weapon against himself. Then came his re-marriage, also forced upon him, lest, after a certain lapse of time, when the scandal had blown over, he should take me again, and I should resume over him the influence I had once exercised, with the political power I had wielded through him. But this act of perfidy on the part of my husband I could not forgive. When almost immediately after his return from London he married Reschid Pasha's sister, he strengthened his political position, but he fell below zero in my estimation, and I steadily refused the secret overtures he afterwards made to me. All I demanded of him were my property and my valuables—of which latter I heard he had made a distribution—or, their equivalent in the shape of an allowance, suitable to my rank. This was the extent of my new demand through Haïda Effendi and Ali Pasha.

My recital to Haïda Effendi was in substance—with the exception of certain political and local details with which he was familiar, but which it was necessary the reader should know—much as I have now given it. I believe it satisfied him on every point, if ever he had entertained a doubt on any.

CHAPTER XXI.

How I came to write a book—How I set about it, and how I fared—The war—We leave Paris for Brussels—Misadventure by the way—An old acquaintance suddenly crops up.

No readier means of covering our expenses occurred to me, on our arrival in Paris, nor of turning to account Haïda Effendi's donation, than furnishing and letting such portions of a house as we ourselves did not require. My speculation, however, proved unsuccessful, and pecuniary difficulties once more set in. My embarrassments augmented as time rolled on, nor did I see any prospect of avoiding a catastrophe. In my dilemma I solicited advice of M. Decourdemanche.

"Why not write a book?" said he. "Yours has been an eventful life; you must have much to relate that would interest the public. What say you to my proposition?"

I had only one objection to make to it; my inability to write any European language. The alternative of dictation offered a **ready solution** of this difficulty, and it was agreed that if his friend Monsieur Paton, of the "Gaulois," could arrange for the publication of the work, in that journal, in a series of *feuilletons*, I might earn a few thousand francs very honourably.

I ought to state that the most pressing necessity alone induced me to yield to this proposition. The idea of writing a book had never once crossed my mind, and I felt great reluctance to make myself the heroine of a romance which turned on details of family life, and involved disclosures I would rather not have to make. There is, however, no reasoning with necessity and clamouring creditors. I therefore yielded to its ignorance of all laws.

Under these circumstances I commenced the dictation of my memoirs, in the form suggested, the eldest son of M. Decourdemanche—whom I shall call Monsieur Alphonse—acting as amanuensis. He devoted about two hours every evening to this work, and as I could not suspect that either he or Monsieur Paton entertained any relations with my husband and his kinsfolk and friends at Constantinople, I kept nothing back. When, however, I asked him to read over what he had written, he would answer that he had taken notes only, and would read them when he had amplified them. This he never did, so that for aught I knew to the contrary, he might have been writing a new version of the Arabian Nights' Entertainment. It was not until long after that I discovered how, through inattention, incapacity, or design, he had distorted facts and misrepresented my motives on several occasions, tending to create an impression of me by no means true or flattering.

The manuscript was completed in almost two months, when he informed me it had been agreed he should submit it to Monsieur Paton for approval. The opinion of this gentleman could not be more favourable than Monsieur Alphonse represented it to be; a piece of intelligence which filled me with pleasant anticipations of being soon relieved of my embarrassments, and remaining with something to the good.

But a bitter disappointment awaited me. A few days later Monsieur Alphonse informed me that Monsieur Paton had taken the manuscript to the Turkish Embassy, and been prevailed upon not to issue the narrative, as originally agreed, but to set the book aside, and write instead, a series of articles on the subject of the intended introduction of the railway system into Turkey, for which the sum of ten thousand francs would be paid him ; and that for the services he had already rendered to the Turkish government, the order of the Medjidi would be conferred upon him. In this way I learnt—to my astonishment—of the relations of Monsieur Paton and his friends with those I had every reason to regard as my enemies, and as spies upon my actions.

I could not get back the manuscript from Monsieur Alphonse, though I importuned him almost daily to return it. At the end of a month he handed me his rough notes, saying he had not had time to amplify them, nor to write out a fair copy. Of course my annoyance and disappointment were extreme, and I did not spare my reproaches; but as the notes —crude though they were—had a certain value, I was glad enough to bring them away.

I at once made application to two other popular daily newspapers, the editor of one of which went so far as to advertise the publication of the work, under the title of "Memoirs of a Turkish Lady." Three or four days after, the editor informed me he had changed his mind, and if he published the work at all, it would not be until the next year. He declined to give me any explanation of his course, and I had to submit to another disappointment. I was also unsuccessful in the other instance, and was so discouraged that I shut up the manuscript in my trunk, and abandoned the idea of publishing it.

I related my failures to Monsieur Alphonse, who suggested that the same occult influences which had been so adverse to me were still in operation to interfere with, and, if possible, destroy, my prospects of success in any undertaking. Do the facts I have related justify such a theory? I have no proofs to cite in support of it. I leave the simple facts to the judgment of the reader.

Without resources, without a prospect of obtaining any, yet clinging desperately to the hope of receiving something from Constantinople, we lived on from day to day, I may say absolutely upon the bounty of the tradespeople of our neighbourhood. My unhappy history had come to their knowledge, and they regarded us with interest and commiseration. The trustfulness of the French is proverbial. Tradespeople will give credit voluntarily, and are not pressing creditors. Evidence of a desire to pay, not unfrequently, as I have experienced, is accepted as cash. I paid as long as I could, and when this was no longer possible, my bare promise to do so as soon as resources came in, was taken in good faith, upon the strength of the honourable discharge of liabilities in the past. I was compelled to leave my neighbourhood considerably in debt; but those to whom I owed knew well the circumstances under which I became their debtor, and, were I to return to it, the good people who trusted me then would do it again if they believed such help as they could give would be likely to aid me.

We were in this position when the declaration of war surprised us, as it did many more. It came upon us as a new and serious trouble, for we had to consider what might be the contingencies of the contest, and to provide for our personal safety.

I had a strange presentiment that the struggle would terminate disastrously for France, and that at the close there would be civil war. As I do not wish to be classed amongst those who are always wise after the event, I abstain from recording the particular reasons which gave this presentiment force, from day to day, and increased my anxiety to leave Paris without delay.

To do this, I felt to be imperative; for I had an instinctive conviction, that if I remained, it would be at imminent personal risk. In a time of turmoil, and in such a city as Paris, my persecutors could not fail to find instruments to their hand, and every facility for carrying out their hostile designs against me, and I was not disposed to afford them the opportunity. Then, as the prospects of victory diminished, a vague sense of alarm began to pervade all ranks, which was not lessened by the culpable reticence of the French Government, and by its more culpable mendacity, when it condescended to give news, relating to the movements of the army on the frontier. The disasters which befel it from the commencement leaked out through the English newspapers and other channels many hours, sometimes days, before the same events were permitted to be recorded in the journals of the capital, and even then the gravest facts were either toned down or altogether ignored. Again, as time wore on, and the catastrophes in the field could no longer be concealed, I observed a singular ferment in the populace, scarcely to be repressed even by the fear of the yet all-powerful police; and here I ask permission to digress a little.

The general opinion here, so far as I have had opportunities of judging, is, that the war declared against Prussia by the Emperor was popular. I am of quite the contrary view. I took some pains to ascertain, from the general bearing of the people, how far their sentiments harmonized with the glowing reports of their enthusiasm for the approaching contest, but failed to discover the unmistakeable signs of its popularity. The outward demonstrations on the Boulevards, the cries of "à Berlin!" and other vociferous manifestations of eagerness for the fray, were not genuine, but were got up for a purpose. Bands of men, lads, boys, women, and girls might always be detected, gathered in small groups here and there in the crowd, all acting in concert. They would, on occasions, set fiercely upon respectable people who expressed an opinion condemnatory of the war, designating them as spies, or Prussians, and hunting them down without mercy. That the poor soldiers whose way to death lay through Paris were warmly received, and conducted to the railway stations with enthusiastic shouts, after being feasted and drenched on their way with cheap beer, indifferent wine, and bad spirits, is perfectly true; but these ovations, natural under the circumstances, were the outward signs of an inward sentiment of gratitude and compassion excited by the spectacle of so many brave men marching to the front to meet the enemy, and in nowise indicated enthusiasm for the war. The leave-taking scenes between parents and their sons were simply heart-rending, and suggested the deepest sorrow on each side. In fact, if the war was popular at all, its popularity was confined to those who—at that time—did not appear likely to suffer from it in any way; and what passed under my own eyes in Paris, from which I derived my impressions, I know to have had its counterpart throughout the empire.

Our equivocal friend, Monsieur Alphonse, had disappeared furtively before the declaration of war. All his father's grand projects had also vanished into the bottomless abyss of impracticable speculations. I saw him one day, towards the end of August, when he informed me that his hopeful heir had become entangled with some undesirable acquaintances, and he had, therefore, despatched the young gentleman to Lisbon with a letter to Marshal Viscount de Saldahna, soliciting some employment under Government. He warned me in a very mysterious manner to avoid all intercourse with Monsieur Alphonse—a warning of which I could not comprehend the signification, as his father's reasons for the injunction were most inconclusive. It was certainly a gratuitous suggestion, as I had lost all interest in the young man. But the old gentleman was keener-sighted than I, and had observed symptoms of a mutual attachment between our two young people. He did not tell me so; but when I discovered the fact, I understood his warning: and the manner of the discovery was this:

Some few days after my strange conversation with Monsieur Decourdemanche, I received from my banker at Constantinople a small sum, being the half-year's interest upon an amount in his hands, belonging to myself, and deposited with him. My uneasiness had then reached its height, and I determined to devote this money to defray our expenses to Brussels. When I communicated my intention to my daughter, she strenuously protested against our quitting Paris; and at last I elicited that she was expecting letters from Monsieur Alphonse, and that, in fact, a strong friendship had sprung up between them. I prevailed upon her, nevertheless, after considerable trouble, to agree to my proposal, and we straightway commenced our preparations for the journey.

I left everything in my apartments for my creditors to make the best of, and took away a few personal effects only, and these absolute necessaries. The march of the Prussians upon Paris was already no longer doubtful; in other words, it was known that it had not been intercepted nor materially impeded by the French Generals. Every precaution was already being taken to prevent the egress of foreigners who had reasons, as I had, for not making their names known to anybody; the line of fortifications was being put into the best condition for defence, and the enrolment of the National Guard had let loose upon Paris a horde of the lowest and most dangerous characters, whose words, looks, and bearing—at least of those I noticed in my quarter—boded no good to the citizens. Everyone was leaving Paris who could do so, and thousands from its vicinity were flocking into it, who had abandoned their homes, terrified at the rapid advance of the enemy. The public sentiment was manifesting itself more strongly every day against the return of the Emperor, and the discussions in the Chamber became daily more hostile to the Government. All these circumstances combined to make me hasten our departure, which took place only two or three days before the overthrow of the Empire by the revolution in Paris.

We were lost in the flock hurrying away northwards, and numbers more joined it on the way. At the Valenciennes station I got out for refreshments, where our journey was arrested in consequence of a mishap, as ludicrous as it was inconvenient. I had wrapped up in a small shawl, which was tied around my waist, a considerable quantity of letters, papers, and other sundries of trifling value. In stepping out of the carriage, the tape which confined the shawl slipped, and out tumbled the contents upon the platform. I was at once surrounded by the railway officials and military on duty, and accused of being a spy. I remonstrated, in vain. My scattered papers were most carefully gathered up, my daughter was compelled to alight, and we were both marched off and conducted to a large room, under an escort numerous and strong enough to have guarded ten men, a crowd following us, and repeating the words, "spies, spies."

The awful tribunal, into the presence of which we were roughly introduced by the shoulders, consisted of the chief of the station, two or three subordinates, certain police agents, and sundry smaller official fry concerned in our capture, and swelling with the glory of it. The dreadful evidences of our guilt were deposited with solemnity upon the table, and our interrogatory commenced.

As I knew the papers were of the most innocent kind, I entertained no apprehension of the issue; but had they been of a compromising character, no protestations of mine would have prevented the inspection of them. I informed my interlocutor that we were Turkish ladies, on our way from Paris to Brussels, and that I would, if they pleased, sit down whilst they examined the papers at their leisure. The judicial assembly was very speedily satisfied that there could not possibly exist any connection between essays on Turkish manners and the harem and Prussian policy; that Haïda Effendi had not selected me to correspond with M. de Moltke concerning the movements of the French troops; and that Ali Pasha and I were not weaving a conspiracy, to be consummated at Brussels, for the capture of the French Emperor, or even for the establishment of a republic instead of the empire. As the signatures were genuine, and the communications were couched in admirably clear French, and as the other papers were of a miscellaneous kind, the letters bearing witness for themselves in our favour, the mistake soon became apparent, and excuses, smiles, and pleasantries took the place of accusations, frowns, and threats. We were forthwith released, and conducted to an hôtel, and resumed our journey by the first train next morning. At the frontier our passports were demanded. Our excuse for not having one was, that we had left Paris hurriedly, quite in a fright, and had not had time to procure one. On the exhibition, however, of Ayesha's certificate of marriage with Questel, as evidence of our identity, we were allowed to pass, and reached Brussels in due course, without any further accident.

We had a friend in this city. His father was my banker at Constantinople; and he kindly assisted us with money, in small sums, as we came to need it. He was also the Turkish Chargé d'Affaires in the Belgian capital.

We had been here about six weeks when our peripatetic friend Monsieur Alphonse suddenly cropped up from Lisbon *viâ* London. He had learnt from his sister of our flight, and now informed us that some friends of his in the British metropolis, who had in hand certain great financial projects had sent for him, requiring his assistance; but as he would have to wait a time until their first scheme should be advanced to a certain point, he had resolved to make Brussels his abiding-place until he was wanted.

Monsieur Alphonse's grand friends did not appear in any hurry to send for him, and whilst they were maturing the projects which were to convert every individual concerned in their promotion into a *millionnaire* at the very least, he was waiting upon Providence and eating dry bread. At the end of three months, and after a long period of silence on the part of his friends, he one day received a letter containing a remittance, and an order for his immediate departure. He leaped at once from the lowest depths of despondency to the sublimest heights of hopefulness, in anticipation of the golden harvest he was called to help gather in, and left us, promising to write to us soon, giving us full particulars of the progress of his fortunes.

I little suspected how intimately we were mixed up with these auriferous dreams.

CHAPTER XXII.

My landlady and "La Lanterne"—An old acquaintance suddenly crops up—We go to London—We get into mysterious company—Our visit to the Turkish Ambassador.

OUR landlady—to whom we were indebted for numerous small acts of kindness, and who seemed never tired of obliging us—suffered from a complaint I do not think is to be found in the medical books, but which I may be permitted to designate as mystery on the brain. She spoke under her voice always, except when she quarrelled with her husband, when its shrill treble would mount to the highest pitch. Her step about the house was velvety as a cat's, and her movements all partook of a feline character. She never entered our apartment nor quitted it without glancing furtively all around, and into every corner of it. She delivered letters as though she had stolen them, and were handing them to a receiver; and when she brought in our food she never failed to scan it suspiciously—though she had prepared it herself—conveying to us the uncomfortable notion that she fancied it might nevertheless be poisoned. Mystery enveloped her as in a fog. I had made up my mind that she had perpetrated some crime, or was in the habit of committing minor misdemeanors, such as smuggling, for she never spoke but in half sentences and riddles, and never appeared completely free from restraint, as if she ever dwelt in fear of some one being on the watch behind her.

One day the conversation having turned upon the ex-Empress, she ranged herself upon the side of this lady's detractors, and lauded Monsieur de Rochefort's "Lanterne" as a model of wit and satire. She had good reason to speak well of it, she said, for it had put a considerable sum of money into her pocket.

The publication in Paris of this venomous pamphlet was—it will be remembered—prohibited, and its author laid under a fine and condemned to a term of imprisonment. The latter he evaded by a flight to Brussels, whence he re-issued the obnoxious print with increased success, and augmented profits, the prohibition having only stimulated its sale. An enormous demand for it arose across the frontier, and thousands of copies thus found their way surreptitiously into France. These were, of course, smuggled over the border, and my landlady was one of the smugglers. Her plan was to enlarge her natural outlines by layers of the "Lanterne," skilfully packed, take her place in the train and discharge cargo, at a given place, into the hands of one of De Rochefort's agents. But a lady, a frequent traveller, whose bulk collapsed every time she returned across the frontier, was a phenomenon not likely long to escape the lynx-eyed police officials, and one of them one day politely requested her presence in an inner room, where a female attendant proceeded to diagnose the seat of the malady productive of such extraordinary symptoms. The result was a shower of "Lanternes," an information, a trial, and three months' imprisonment; a mild penalty considering that the legal one by special command was a term of years in the hulks. Our landlady got off as she did by pleading ignorance of the character of the book, and of the law prohibiting its introduction into France. She fortunately had to deal with a tribunal individually addicted to read the national politics by the glimmer of the "Lanterne."

My judgment of her was, therefore, correct. She dabbled in smuggling; hence her mysterious airs.

Within a week after Monsieur Alphonse's arrival in London, we received a letter informing us that he was lying dangerously ill in the house of a friend, who was also his employer and patron, and that the greatest doubts of his recovery were entertained.

This news caused us much uneasiness. We had become accustomed to the society of Monsieur Alphonse, and we believed in his friendship, for he had never given us cause to call his loyalty in question. In the affair of my book, he had acted only as an intermediary, he being in the hands of his patron, Monsieur Paton, and when I came to learn—upon his authority—that his failure to make a fair copy of his notes, according to agreement, was due to the pressure of other duties upon which his daily bread depended, I felt inclined to pity rather than to blame him, notwithstanding that I was made the victim of his negligence. Under these circumstances, to wish ourselves near him at a moment when his life seemed in danger, was a most natural impulse, and the transition to the thought of making an endeavour to get to him was not less so. I remembered too, the strong recommendation of the Turkish Ambassador at Piræus, reiterated by his colleagues at Corfu, that we should go to London, and now that a real motive for the journey had sprung up, I began to consider seriously whether we might not, after all, as well act upon the suggestion. Further, I still hoped my husband's obduracy might at last yield to my importunity, on our daughter's account, and the good offices of the Turkish Ambassador in London seemed to me likely to be of service, if I could only prevail upon him to interfere in our behalf. Having considered the matter very fully, I finally resolved to make the venture.

On the very day of our departure I was astounded by the sudden appearance of Mustapha-Djehad. He had come from Venice, after serving three years in the Papal Zouaves, and he, like ourselves, was without resources. I had no alternative but to take him with us, though his presence added to the embarrassment of my position.

It was late—ten o'clock at night—when we reached the Victoria Station. Not knowing whither to go, and having only the address of Monsieur Alphonse, we called a coach and showed the driver the paper on which the direction was written. This individual, thoroughly imbued with the traditions of his class, took the fullest advantage of our being strangers, and ignorant of the topography of the metropolis, by indulging us in a ride which lasted until midnight, when he landed us at the foot of a steep street, somewhere on the south side of London; but not until I had harangued him at a rate which attracted the attention of a benevolent policeman, who soon relieved the embarrassment of our erratic coachman as to the direction in which he ought to take us.

At last he stopped in front of a fine house—one of a terrace—into which I entered, alone, and asked to see Monsieur Alphonse. I did not choose to give my own name, but my voice was recognised by the invalid who occupied a large sitting-room on the ground floor, converted into a bed room for his special use. I found him in bed, but the well-furnished apartment was brilliantly illuminated, and he was surrounded by four of his male friends, who eyed me with apparent indifference when I entered, but whom I detected scrutinizing me narrowly when they fancied I was not observing them.

Monsieur Alphonse appeared to me to be remarkably lively for a man at the point of death, the only indication of illness that I could perceive being a spotty redness of the face, as of measles or scarlet fever, though he was not suffering from either of these complaints. His surprise on seeing me was undisguised, but he said that his intention had been to invite us to pay a visit to London as soon as convalescence set in. He introduced me to one of his friends present, a tall handsome man of some thirty years of age, with fierce owl-eyes, whose fixed glare made me uncomfortable. This individual—whom I will call Monsieur Henri—saluted me with stiff courtesy, and Monsieur Alphonse then confided us to the care of Monsieur Henri, who, he said, would see us comfortably provided for till morning.

I do not know to what hotel our new guide had us conducted. It was a grand establishment, and I believe it to have been in the immediate vicinity of the station whence we had come. We were accommodated in splendid style; but haunted by the spectral eyes which had been fixed on me during our drive to the hotel, I could not sleep, though ill from fatigue and excitement.

Who was this Monsieur Henri? Who were his companions? Why were they so deeply interested in Monsieur Alphonse's recovery? I remembered their physiognomies, and the mingled expression of alarm and suspicion these wore. Monsieur Alphonse was not in so critical a state as to need four anxious male attendants at his bedside, and a midnight consultation on business matters was, to say the least of it, open to suspicion. Then, on the way to the hotel,

Monsieur Henri assured me, in confidential tones, that he would not abandon Monsieur Alphonse, but would give him permanent and good employment, and be his stanch friend, happen what might. What could be the relations between these two men, that Monsieur Henri should assume the airs and the tone of the patron of Monsieur Alphonse, and at the same time be waiting upon him as a tender nurse? Was any plot a-foot for the accomplishment of which the latter was an indispensable instrument? I could not divine, but my suspicions were seriously awakened, and my conclusions took an unfavourable direction.

Next morning a messenger arrived from Monsieur Henri, who re-conducted us to a furnished house, contiguous to the one in which lay his friend Monsieur Alphonse, and we were told to make ourselves at home in it; but how to do this without money was not even suggested.

I lost no time in seeking an audience of the Ambassador of the Sublime Porte, who, when he saw Ayesha, wept freely, and besought her and me to return to Constantinople. We adhered to our resolution, so many times affirmed, not to trust ourselves within the limits of an empire, to the furthermost corners of which the power of my husband extended. The Ambassador then advised my daughter to write a letter to her father, setting forth her privations and her position, and appealing to his paternal affection to rescue her from it; but she was on no account to mention the name of her adviser, and he declined to give us any reason for a reticence which appeared to me inexplicable.

Had he told me, what he then knew, that his friend Kibrizli-Mehemet Pasha—to whom he was sincerely attached—lay at that moment ill of a mortal malady; that on seeing Ayesha, he wept at the thought that her father would die without embracing her; that it was under these circumstances he advised our return to Constantinople, I should have risked all consequences, and acted upon his suggestion, and upon the natural impulses of my own heart.

Ayesha agreed to follow his advice, assuring his Excellency that she had never lost her affection for her father, but that her experience of his cruelty had terrified her. He had exiled her, had persecuted her whilst she was in her own country, and she had fled before a threat of his to imprison her for life in a subterranean dungeon. She would gladly embrace him at that moment, for she still loved him.

We got Monsieur Alphonse to write this letter, and we took it to the Embassy, as the best channel for conveying it to its destination. Here all kinds of objections were raised to enclosing it in the official bag, but these were finally overcome, and we left under the impression that it would be forwarded. Whether this was done I know not, but no reply to it ever reached us.

CHAPTER XXIII.

Monsieur Alphonse and his friends—Singular and suspicious incidents—One of my husband's body-guard turns up in an unexpected manner—Last visit to the Turkish Ambassador—I determine to go away—Scene with my daughter—We part.

THE convalescence of Monsieur Alphonse, which commenced at the end of a month, altered our position. The small amount of ready money I had brought with me was quite exhausted, and no news came in from Constantinople. I had fortunately been relieved of one burden through the kindness of Madame Davidoff, who paid Mustapha-Djehad's expenses to Paris where he found employment, of a kind, through her interest. Our position did not improve, as the days rolled on, and was at its worst when Monsieur Alphonse proposed to me to take a house and let him apartments in it. The project commended itself to me under an economical aspect, and we removed without delay into a suitable dwelling in the immediate neighbourhood.

I never learnt what matters engaged Monsieur Alphonse's time and attention, nor what were the grand projects he and his associates were constantly considering and discussing in secret conclave. Shortly after our installation, despatches, telegrams, registered letters, and others in quantities began to arrive, which he conveyed morning and evening to his patron. In answer to our questions, he used to say these communications related to financial operations of immense importance, and that if they succeeded, his own share would be enormous, and then he would leave the country. Whenever I and my daughter visited at Monsieur Henri's—for his wife and his mother dwelt in the house—we always found that he was closeted with Monsieur Alphonse and some eight or ten others, and their deliberations would often last until long after midnight. The absence of any other ladies but those I have mentioned, and the constant attendance of the few gentlemen associated with Monsieur Henri — no others ever visiting at the house—impressed me very unfavourably, and I set the whole party down, in my own mind, as a gang of adventurers, living upon the gullibility of an easily deluded public.

Monsieur Alphonse was a frequent visitor to the city, where his patron had an office. I also discovered he often went to the Ottoman Embassy. Leaving it one day, I saw him come out, but pretended not to do so, and passed on. He concealed his face when he perceived me, and ran behind a lamp-post. The circumstance was suspicious. He had never once hinted a word of his having any connection with the Legation; but even had this been the case, and his purpose an honest one, he could have no motive for concealment. I suppose he felt he had placed himself in a false position, and feared I should speak to my daughter of this strange incident, for he could not be sure I had not seen him. I was, therefore, not surprised when Ayesha told me he had informed her, that having been overtaken by a shower of rain, close by the Legation, he had run in there for shelter. I laughed at her simplicity, told her there had been no rain, and that Monsieur Alphonse had invented the shower to impose upon her credulity, and to forestall any inquiry of mine why he had been at the Legation at all.

Another time he brought news that if I had not been with my daughter, the Pasha, my husband, would long since have made Ayesha an allowance, but his fury against me was so great, that so long as she remained with me, he would not give her a farthing. He made this communication confidentially to Ayesha, adding that he had obtained the intelligence from some Pasha, newly come from Constantinople. I ascertained that no such personage had arrived, and as the main fact was indisputable, I had a right to conclude the information had been derived from a higher authority.

Still another incident. One morning he received a telegram, which he opened and partly read. So far as he did so it was to the effect that if he succeeded in "that business, the decoration of the Medji—" here he stopped short, stammered and corrected his slip of the tongue by saying: "no, no; how stupid of me; a decoration from the King of Portugal, I should have read."

As Monsieur Alphonse already wore at his button-hole a riband of some Portuguese order, the promise of a second did not appear probable. Moreover, there was no mistaking his reference to that of the Medjidi, nor his confusion and embarrassment at having betrayed himself in the exuberance of his delight at the prospect of this equivocal honour. I was not deceived, and from this moment no longer doubted that he was in communication with those unfriendly to me at Constantinople.

That I also dwelt in personal danger from them

was brought home to me about this time, by another circumstance.

I was taking a walk in our neighbourhood with a friend, when I noticed a common-looking Turk following us. Presently he passed us, and I at once recognized him as one of my husband's followers. He came from Adrianople, and was one of the most desperate of ruffians, who had earned a fearful reputation in the country as a robber and an assassin. He was captured at last, and brought before the Pasha, my husband, and would have been hanged at once if the Pasha had not taken him into his service, on the promise of good behaviour for the future.

I may record, as illustrative of Turkish customs, that the governors of provinces and officials invested with arbitrary authority, are privileged to save the life of a criminal, upon a promise of this kind, and to employ him as a thief-taker, or in any similar capacity. Such men are usually taken into the service of their benefactor, who holds them—on pain of death by a summary process—to their promise not to rob nor murder, nor to commit any misdemeanor: but his command to them is law.

I determined to speak to this ruffian, who, when I stopped him, regarded me with eyes flaming with ferocity. He recognized me though he did not address me by name, and I took care not to betray myself. He said he had arrived only a few days before; he had come over to see the country: he had not been to the Legation, and did not know the Ambassador. He asked me if the lady by my side was my daughter: a singular question if I had been a stranger to him, for he could have no interest in the fact, but it was one of great significance in the present instance, implying foreknowledge, and seeing that he asked no other question. I met him a second time, some days later, when, upon sight of me, he ran into a news-shop and sat down on a chair behind the door. I followed him in—my friend being with me—and challenged him upon his mode of seeing the country by prowling about in one neighbourhood. He answered not a word, but went crimson in the face, and hung his head. Satisfied at having confronted him, and with a vivid impression of the nature of his errand, I went out, resolved to take a decisive step.

I paid another visit to the Turkish Ambassador, and solicited him to help me to funds sufficient to enable me to rejoin my eldest daughter in Venice. His Excellency urged me not to quit the country, for he knew very positively, was, in fact, sure, that within a few days I should receive a reply from my husband. Thus assured, and upon such high authority, I renounced the idea of my journey into Italy.

Still the days passed and nothing came, and the incidents I have detailed having aggravated my apprehensions and confirmed my convictions of imminent personal danger, I felt that my own safety could be insured only by flight. I was also strongly influenced by a desire to disentangle myself from the vicious circle in which Monsieur Alphonse and his associates moved. I had no proofs of their being engaged in nefarious transactions, but the mystery which enveloped them and their proceedings, the dark words which continually fell from the lips of Monsieur Alphonse, and the tone and manners of the whole band, amply justified the unfavourable opinion I entertained of the parties, and left me no alternative but to sever the connection at once, if I desired to preserve my own self-respect.

I communicated my views and intentions to my daughter, not doubting she would be prepared to accompany me anywhere. To my utter amazement she replied to the reasons I gave her for taking this step, by ridiculing me for entertaining apprehensions purely imaginary, and by stating that if I went away she should remain. I remonstrated with her upon the impropriety of her course, and pointed out the result. She retorted that she was quite old enough to take care of herself, and people might comment upon her conduct as they pleased. In a word, a scene too painful to my feelings to describe resulted from this conversation. She was obdurate, and turned a deaf ear to reason. I was obstinate, because I felt I was right in condemning the imprudence of my daughter in exposing herself to the scandalous reports which must result from her remaining in the house after I had quitted it, and because I also felt that my self-respect was involved as well as my personal safety, and that between these and an undutiful caprice on the part of my daughter, I could not consent to any compromise. Under such circumstances, no medium course was possible, and I therefore acted upon my conviction of what was right.

The predominant feeling in my heart that night was of complete abandonment. No mother ever loved a daughter with an affection exceeding my own; none had sacrificed more for one than I had done for her. I had endured the loss of position, property, friends, consideration; had undergone the excess of privation, submitted to all kinds of humiliation, to vexations of spirit without end, and for what, at the last? ingratitude, contempt of reputation, deliberate desertion! The struggle between my motherly love and my sense of right and propriety was terrible, but I could not bring myself to come back upon a decision my conscience approved.

I rose quite early the next morning, heart-broken, weary, ill. The streets were unpeopled, the night-lamps were not yet extinguished, everything seemed dead, and responded to the death in my heart. I gathered up the few effects I could take away, and instinctively took a step or two in the passage leading to my child's room. Then I hesitated. The impulse to look at her once more ere I quitted her, perhaps for ever, was strong as nature, but I resisted it. I should disturb her with my kisses, and I remembered, too, her defiant look and carriage the previous night, and her unkind, undutiful, ungrateful words. I stifled my sobs, turned away from the door of her bed-chamber, and staggered rather than walked out of the house.

Yet, not until I found myself in the street, with the cool air fanning my burning cheek and eyes, did I truly realize that I was alone in the world.

CHAPTER XXIV.

The last blow.

I MADE the best of my way to the residence of the friend to whom I have already alluded, surprising her considerably by my early arrival. But for her kindness and sympathy I think I must have died. We concluded it would be desirable for me to take change and rest, and we proceeded the same day to the sea-side.

If I were to say that during our brief stay my heart became less sensitive to its loss, I should be misleading the reader. Nature, however, has endowed the mind with an elastic faculty which enables it to bear the shock of the heaviest misfortunes, and to recover from it more or less speedily, whilst retaining its consciousness of calamity. But for this faculty, it must infallibly give way under the poignant anguish of a heavy visitation. So was it with me. I could not throw off my deep grief. I could not dismiss my darling child from my thoughts; but my bleeding heart begun to reconcile itself to the consciousness of separation from its idol, finding comfort and consolation in the knowledge that its loved object still lived, and that a reunion was not impossible.

With respect to my own prospects, I had lost all hope, now, of help from my husband. I placed no reliance on the assurances that a communication from the Pasha was on its way to me, fixing my settlement. How came the fact to be known, I had asked myself, and what had brought about such a change in the Pasha's sentiments towards me? My conviction was that I was being cajoled, and that the recommendations to patience were of a piece with former suggestions, plausible in form and substance, but delusive, hollow, false in reality. In my greater trouble at the loss of my daughter, I thought little of what was to become of myself. I seemed to need only to be left alone to indulge in the sorrow which was breaking me down, yet which seemed to me a luxury. I had staked upon my child the sum of what remained to me of happiness, but fortune had deceived me, and all was lost; save this sorrow at my heart.

We had been about a fortnight absent, and I was

beginning to recover from the first bitterness of grief. My friend, knowing how deep an interest I took in Turkish affairs, usually read the telegrams from Constantinople before any other intelligence. One morning, on looking over the newspaper, she suddenly uttered a loud exclamation, and cast the paper down. She could scarcely reply to my inquiry as to the cause of her emotion, but at length gasped out the words:

"Oh, Madame, dear Madame! Your husband is dead. The telegram says that he died after a long and lingering malady."

My blood ran cold: my head swam; I fainted. On recovering myself, tears came to my relief. Death extinguishes all animosities, and at this moment I lost sight of the sufferings I had endured at the hands of the Pasha, and remembered only the husband I had loved tenderly, who had loved me passionately, and with whom I had passed so many years of my young life. From the bottom of my heart I forgave him all the ill he had done me, and even found excuses for him, for—paradoxical as it may seem—I knew that the source of his cruel displeasure and of his persecution lay in his intense love for me, diverted from its channel—through his own weakness—by the intrigues and misrepresentations of those who surrounded him, and who had an interest in placing an abyss between us.

I sincerely trust God will forgive me the ill I may have done in my life-time as fully as I do Kibrizli. I have, however, no forgiveness in my heart for those who listened to the revengeful ravings of a man—burning with love for his daughter whom he had lost, and irritated by a malady which left him scarcely a respite from intense suffering—and took advantage of them to persecute me up to the time of his death, and to this present moment, their aim being the advancement of their own selfish ends.

But this intelligence also brought with it a revelation. What had been dark, suddenly became clear. All at once it broke in upon me that my daughter and I had been duped by Monsieur Alphonse and his friends, their ultimate object being to secure the Pasha's wealth through Ayesha. Here was the plot.

Through their friends at Constantinople and at the various Ottoman Legations, and through their spies, they had heard of the Pasha's illness, and of its hopeless character; so declared from the moment his malady reached its final stage.

His wealth was notoriously enormous, and was—

as I have already stated—coveted by his rapacious male next of kin, amongst whom it would be distributed in the absence of direct heirs. If Mustapha-Djehad could be proved illegitimate—that is, only an adopted child of the Pasha's—the bulk of the inheritance would revert to Ayesha. If the lad's legitimacy were established, three-fourths of the inheritance would be his, and the remainder Ayesha's. Now, the Pasha had over and over again deposed to the legitimacy of Mustapha, and had even driven out with violence, sundry of his colleagues in the government, who had ventured to trouble him with a repetition of the rumours his relatives had circulated concerning the parentage of the young man. He had also made a similar declaration in writing. Thus, before these harpies could secure Mustapha's share of the inheritance, they would have to establish his illegitimacy as an adopted child; but so long as I could enter on the scene against them, their chances of success were reduced to the slenderest proportions, for who could gainsay my word, and overthrow my proofs, sustained as they would have been, by the verbal and written acknowledgment of the Pasha! Hence the intrigues to get rid of me, and to impair, by every means, the validity of my testimony : intrigues stimulated by Kibrizli's own, to revenge himself upon me for quitting Turkey with our daughter.

I had not, myself, anything to expect from the Pasha's inheritance, and had never demanded but what was my own, of right, or its equivalent. Ayesha's portion, however—immense, if Mustapha-Djehad's legitimacy were disproved; and much can be done in Turkey, by a judicious distribution of bribes; would still be considerable enough, in the contrary contingency, to render her a grand prize to whomsoever could secure control over her. Here, again, I stood in the way, so that to all parties I was an obstacle to the success of their designs, and all had a direct interest in disposing of me somehow. It is simply marvellous how I have escaped from such an unscrupulous band.

Ayesha's own folly now left her at the mercy of those who had for so many months sought to entangle her in their snares. One of their objects had been to isolate her from me, but all their machinations in this direction had failed, and were likely to fail so long as I watched over her. My apprehensions for her safety were now again excited to the last degree by the intelligence of my husband's death, and I could not rest until I had once more seen her, and made her acquainted with the event which so affected her prospects. Accordingly I and my friend hastened to the house I had so recently quitted, but to our surprise, we found it vacated, and in charge of a strange woman.

"Madam," said she, in reply to my inquiry what had become of my daughter, "your daughter was married about ten days ago to Monsieur Alphonse. He received news of her husband's death, and they were married immediately after. I don't know where they are."

This was the last blow. The cup was full. Husband, daughter, wealth, position, prospects, gone! I turned sick! Hope died within me: smitten out of my heart suddenly, at once, by this final stroke. The bitterness of the hour was aggravated by the thought that my enemies had at length triumphed, and were rejoicing over my defeat. I felt that nothing now remained to me that I at all cared to live for. Bewildered, scarcely conscious, I allowed my friend to lead me away, like a passive infant. She took me back to the sea-side, where a raging fever seized me, and where, for a period of five months, I hung between lunacy and death.

It was my fate to recover. With convalescence came thoughts for the means of supplying the necessaries of existence. I remembered the rough record of my life, lying useless in my trunk. I had no ambition to appear before the world as an author, but daily needs are imperative, and my sole, immediately available resource lay in that trunk. I sought a publisher, and found one. I leave "Thirty Years in the Harem" and this present narrative of my experiences in Europe to tell their own tale. Their sole merit is their truthfulness. Between me and my persecutors I leave the reader as Judge.

THE END.

www.ingramcontent.com/pod-product-compliance
Lightning Source LLC
Chambersburg PA
CBHW030006240426
43672CB00007B/848